Zodiac Puzzles

for Scroll Saw Woodworking

Judy and Dave Peterson

Fox Chapel
Publishing

Dedication

We dedicate this book
to our grandchildren,
Nico and 'Lyssa Peterson.

ISBN 978-1-56523-393-5

Library of Congress Cataloging-in-Publication Data

Peterson, Judy (Judith S.)

Zodiac puzzles for scroll saw woodworking / by Judy and Dave Peterson. -- 1st ed.

p. cm.

Includes index.

ISBN 978-1-56523-393-5

1. Jig saws. 2. Woodwork--Patterns. 3. Zodiac in art. I. Peterson, Dave (David S.) II. Title.

TT186.P4674 2009

745.51'3--dc22

2008046139

To learn more about the other great books from Fox Chapel Publishing, or to find a retailer near you, call toll-free 800-457-9112 or visit us at *www.FoxChapelPublishing.com*.

Note to Authors: We are always looking for talented authors to write new books in our area of woodworking, design, and related crafts. Please send a brief letter describing your idea to Acquisition Editor, 1970 Broad Street, East Petersburg, PA 17520.

Printed in China
First printing: April 2009

Table of Contents

Introduction

Capricorn Step-by-Step, 12/22–1/19, page 12

Year of the Horse Step-by-Step, 2002, page 46

Throughout the years, people worldwide have been fascinated with the mysterious mythology of the zodiac. The idea that the time of your birth could affect your personality, and that it is possible to estimate the results of your interactions with others based on that information, has a great allure to many. Artists, especially, seem drawn to the creative possibilities offered by the characters of the zodiac. You are holding in your hands the newest creative twist on the zodiac: *Zodiac Puzzles for Scroll Saw Woodworking*. Included are instructions for creating 30 beautiful freestanding puzzles from Western and Eastern tradition, along with interesting astrological information and beautiful historical star maps. Here's what you'll find inside:

Step-by-Steps

Two detailed, photo-filled step-by-steps are included to guide you through cutting and finishing your first puzzles. The Western zodiac project, Capricorn, illuminates the process of scrolling thick wood. Also included are instructions on setting wire, nails, and jewels into your puzzle to show the sign's star pattern. This advanced puzzle takes Judy about 60 to 75 minutes to cut, about 15 minutes to sand, and about 10 minutes to finish. Adding the gems and wires takes about an additional hour. When you get this project down, you'll be able to cut any other puzzle in the book. The Eastern zodiac project, Year of the Horse, explains how to create a colorful tray puzzle that looks like a Chinese brush painting. Judy can cut one of these intermediate puzzles in about 60 minutes. Detailed instructions are included to guide you through the use of watercolor crayons and wood stains to finish the puzzle. Both projects include a pattern, full-page reference photograph of the finished project, creative source material, and personality information.

Western zodiac projects

All 12 of the Western zodiac signs are represented here as fantastic puzzle projects. Each project includes: a pattern—complete with star placement, full-page reference photograph of the finished project, historic star map, lore, and astrology. Basic background information and history of the Western zodiac is also given.

Aries, 3/21–4/19, page 22

Taurus, 4/20–5/20, page 24

Gemini, 5/21–6/20, page 26

Cancer, 6/21–7/22, page 28

Leo, 7/23–8/22, page 30

Virgo, 8/23–9/22, page 32

Libra, 9/23–10/22, page 34

Scorpio, 10/23–11/21, page 36

Sagittarius, 11/22–12/21, page 38

Aquarius, 1/20–2/18, page 40

Pisces, 2/19–3/20, page 42

Introduction

Eastern zodiac projects

Each of the 12 Eastern zodiac animals is shown here as a beautiful puzzle, all inspired by original Chinese brush paintings—which are also included for your reference. Each project includes: a pattern, full-page reference photograph of the finished project, original Chinese brush painting, and personality information. Basic background information and history of the Eastern zodiac is also given. Note: The first year of each animal in the twenty-first century is listed below. Please consult the chart on page 94 for a listing of all the years since 1900.

Rat, 2008, page 52

Ox, 2009, page 54

Tiger, 2010, page 56

Rabbit, 2011, page 58

Dragon, 2000, page 60

Snake, 2001, page 62

Ram, 2003, page 64

Monkey, 2004, page 66

Rooster, 2005, page 68

Dog, 2006, page 70

Pig, 2007, page 72

Constellations

As a bonus, six of the most popular constellations in the night sky have also been included as puzzle projects. Each project includes: a pattern—complete with star placement, full-page reference photograph of the finished project, historic star map, and lore. Basic background information about constellations is also given.

Ursa Major, page 76

Orion, page 78

Cassiopeia, page 80

Cepheus, page 82

Andromeda, page 84

Perseus, page 86

Appendix

The Tools & Techniques section (page 89) includes everything you need to know to be able to scroll, sand, and finish any puzzle. The practice pattern includes all of the techniques you need to know to cut any pattern in this book. Safety guidelines are also included. The Index at the back of the book will help you find the pattern you're looking for (page 95).

About the Authors

A former schoolteacher and librarian, Judy found her niche in life as a woodworker. She bought her first saw in 1990 and, within the first six months, was cutting and creating her own designs. A winner of many design awards, Judy now sells her puzzles at art and craft shows around the country. Together with her husband, Dave, she has written numerous articles for *Scroll Saw Woodworking & Crafts*, and she teaches scroll sawing at the Woodcraft store in her hometown of Madison, Wisconsin. In her spare time, Judy reads, keeps track of politics on TV, gardens, cooks, turns bowls on her lathe, and puts together other people's flat puzzles.

Dave is officially retired after a career in programming and systems analysis. His interest in and experience with computers, databases, and spreadsheets make him suited to run the record-keeping side of Judy's small business.

In his spare time, Dave reads, is active in the local Macintosh Users' Group, writes the occasional article for the Wisconsin Alliance of Artists and Craftspeople newsletter, and tries to keep up with his wife.

As far as their books and magazine articles go, Judy does all the designing, scrollwork, sanding, and finishing. She also writes all the technical portions. Dave organizes the material, provides a first-draft version for Judy's review, takes the in-process photos, does all of the typing, and interfaces with their editor. All in all, the distribution of duties capitalizes on both their strengths and provides an amicable distribution of labor.

Judy and Dave co-authored an article in the Summer 2005 issue of *Scroll Saw Workshop* magazine, titled "How to Select the Shows and Design your Booth for Maximum Sales."

This book is the result of their fourth collaboration. Fox Chapel Publishing published their first book, *Dinosaur Puzzles for the Scroll Saw*, in August 2002, their second book, *Fantasy & Legend Puzzles for the Scroll Saw*, in February 2005, and their third book, *Animal Puzzles for the Scroll Saw: Second Edition*, in October 2008.

Preface

Why interlocking & freestanding puzzles?

I like puzzles. These days, when I'm not making my own puzzles, I'm likely to be doing someone else's. I didn't, however, plan to go into business designing and making jigsaw puzzles. I bought a scroll saw because I have always liked wood and because I was fascinated by the scroll saw work I saw at an art show. In 1989, when my family and I made our annual trek to a nearby Renaissance Fair, I bought a five-piece puzzle as a souvenir. While it was attractive, it was not interlocking, so you really couldn't pick it up without having it fall apart.

When I began designing my own puzzles, I decided all of them would be interlocking so they could be handled. The puzzles in this book reflect that decision I made in 1990—all of them are interlocking. That means once you have the puzzles in a standing position, you can pick them up by any piece and turn them completely around without having them fall apart. But, you have to make sure you keep them vertical and don't tip them!

The first project I cut out when I brought home that wonderful new toy, my first scroll saw, was a three-piece rabbit. As a woodworker of long standing, I used lumber I had in my workshop. It was an old piece of 1" x 4" pine. One of the things I liked about the puzzle was it was thick enough to stand. The concept of a freestanding puzzle stayed with me as I moved on to using hardwoods.

Why zodiac creatures?

There were several incidents that sparked the creation of this book. The first was when an acquaintance saw some of my puzzles and asked if I could do a puzzle for him. I said, "Probably–what kind?" He appeared embarrassed, said, "Now don't take this wrong or anything, but could you make a puzzle of this?" At that point, he pulled up his shirt. His astrological sign, Taurus, was tattooed on his stomach. That was the beginning…thanks, Paul! Customers and friends seemed interested in more puzzles of the zodiac, so I obliged.

Another acquaintance suggested jewelling the star patterns onto the puzzle—consequently, all twelve of the Western zodiac and all six of the constellation patterns include markings that show the stars making up the constellation. If you really want to get fancy, or make a memorable birthday gift, you could use birthstone stud earrings as two of the stars. I like to use crystals to mark the prominent stars and bits of silver wire for smaller stars. Stainless steel finishing nails are another option for marking stars.

When I started looking for the star patterns I ran across some very good reference books with alternate stories and designs (see the bibliography). But that was still only twelve patterns and you need about thirty for a book.

Then my friend, Charlotte, turned up with her Year of the Horse painting at an art show and it all came together. Twelve signs of the Western zodiac plus twelve Eastern zodiac animals left only six others to include. I chose some of the most familiar constellations. Almost everyone can find Ursa Major, the Great Bear (a.k.a. the Big Dipper), Orion, and Cassiopeia. And if you have Queen Cassiopeia, you may as well include the King, the Princess, and the Hero.

Add a step-by-step to show the freestanding puzzle style and one to show how to make an easy painted tray puzzle, interesting information about the personality of each sign, lore about each constellation, and plenty of helpful tips, and you've got yourself another book. Happy cutting!

Judy and Dave

1 The Western Zodiac

The zodiac is an area of the night sky that holds twelve constellations. This belt is located a few degrees above and below the ecliptic plane—the path that the sun appears to follow through the sky. In astrology, each of the signs of the zodiac is said to rule a portion (approximately one-twelfth) of the solar year. This belief seems to have started in ancient Mesopotamia more than 5,000 years ago. The signs of the Western zodiac are important to modern astrology, which says the sign you were born under exerts a great influence over your behavior and circumstances.

Follow along as the Capricorn step-by-step section shows how to cut a thick freestanding puzzle, sand it, and insert star markers if desired. Following are the rest of the Western zodiac patterns, arranged chronologically. Aries, which starts in mid-March, is traditionally the first sign of the zodiac.

Each puzzle includes more than just a pattern and photo of the completed project. The common pictorial symbol for each sign is given, along with the dates associated with the sign and a brief description of each personality. A beautiful historic star map, created in the 1600s by Polish astronomer Johannes Hevelius, is also shown for each constellation. Finally, the Greek or Roman mythology for each constellation is included.

Image courtesy of Micheletb.

The zodiac has always captured the creative imagination of artists. These woodcuts were created in the sixteenth century.

Note: It was common for early astronomers to draw their star maps from a viewpoint outside of the celestial sphere, whereas today our star maps reflect a viewpoint from inside, as seen from Earth. Please note that the images from Johannes Hevelius' star maps will appear to have reversed star patterns and are placed as they appear in the sky.

The Western Zodiac – Advanced Pattern

English sycamore, 6½" (165mm) high.

♑ **Capricorn:**
The Sea Goat

December 22–January 19

The Capricorn personality is, above all, practical. Those born under this sign tend to be hardworking, ambitious, and realistic, a combination that leads to successful careers. Capricorns are also resourceful, disciplined, trustworthy, and intelligent. They appreciate high quality and are sensitive to beauty.

In mythology, the sea goat was created when the god Pan, in goat form, leapt into a river and started to transform into a fish. But the river wasn't deep enough, so he only transformed his back half, thereby ending with a goat head and a fish tail.

Note: The step-by-step photos in this section, except for the lower right photos on pages 18 and 19, were taken at the Fox Chapel Publishing studio. Ben Fink cut the puzzle, and Scott Kriner photographed.

Setup

Before you can cut a puzzle out, of course, you must select the board you want to use. Examine both sides of the board carefully, looking for bad spots, including checks, knotholes, and obvious internal cracks. Mark these flaws on the top of your board. I use a wide, black permanent marker for this task.

Make a copy of the Capricorn pattern and decide where to position it on the board. Avoid the bad spots when positioning your pattern. Spray the pattern with repositionable spray adhesive and apply the pattern to the board.

Be sure the adhesive you choose is "repositionable." If the label on a product doesn't include that word, you don't want to use that product for this purpose. The bond from a non-repositionable adhesive will be so secure that you'll have to spend time sanding the pattern off the pieces. However, patterns glued with repositionable spray adhesive usually peel off, leaving no residue. The longer you wait to peel the pattern off, the harder it will be to do so. I've had good luck with Duro All-Purpose Spray Adhesive, available at K-Mart and Wal-Mart stores, as well as many lumberyards.

As you probably know, scroll saw blades come in sizes from 2 through 12—the lower the number, the finer the teeth. For 4/4 boards, I use a #7 blade. This allows the pieces to move freely.

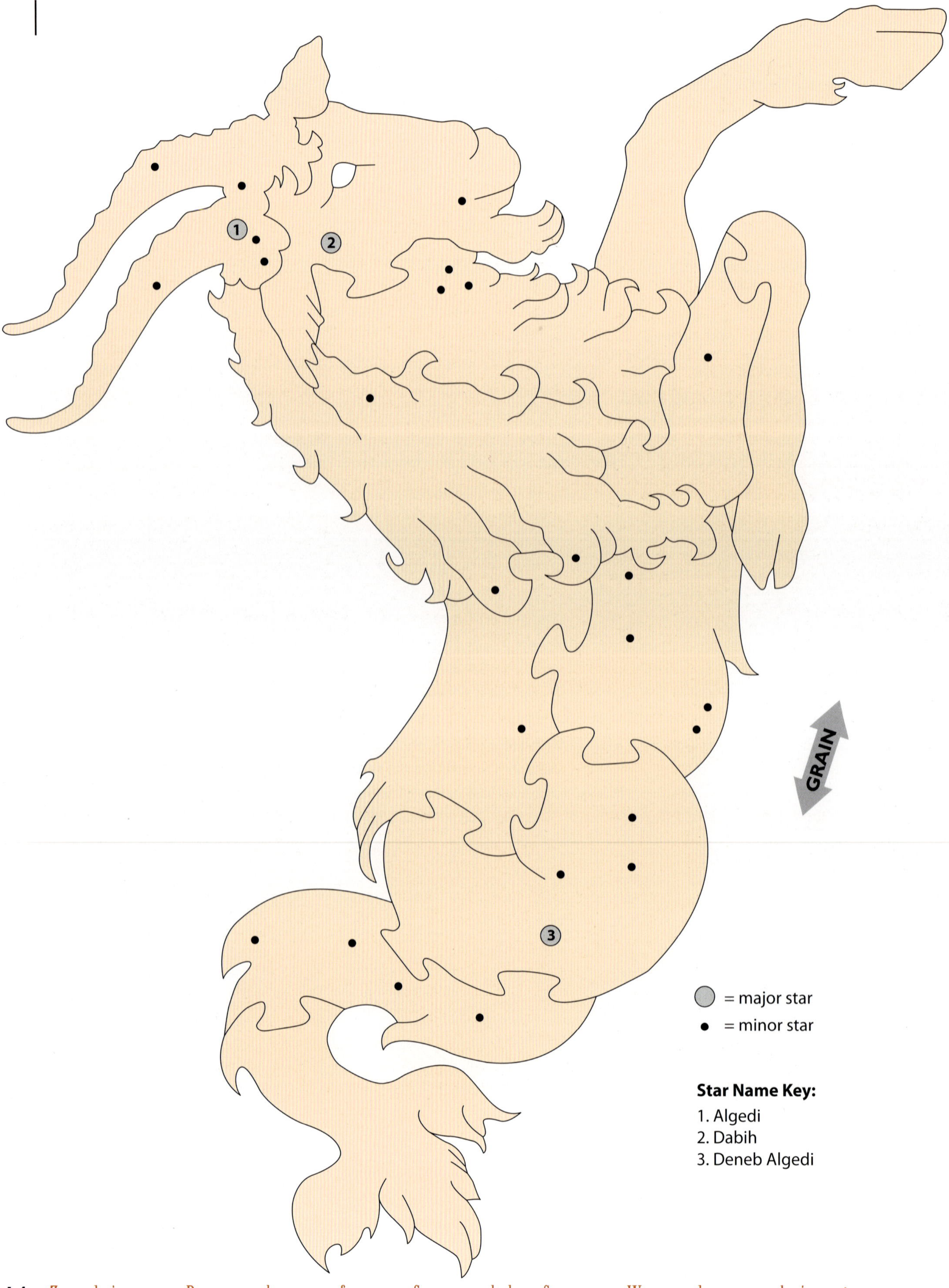

Star Name Key:

1. Algedi
2. Dabih
3. Deneb Algedi

Tools and Materials

- Scroll saw with dust blower
- Skip tooth or reverse tooth blades (#7)
- Spray adhesive
- Square
- Clear 2" (50mm) packing tape
- Sanding method of choice
- Flat trays
- Glue box
- Metal tray
- Dip and drip-dry equipment
- Paper towels
- Resealable gallon plastic bags
- Nitrile gloves
- Rubber fingertips
- A board of appropriate dimensions and approximately 4/4" (25mm) thickness
- ¼" (6mm) tear drop bit

Note: *These are the tools I use. However, feel free to use the supplies and tools of your choice.*

Section 1: Cutting the puzzle

1 The first step is to drill whatever holes you're going to drill before you start cutting. You may not want to drill the holes representing the star pattern, but you should at least drill the hole through which you must cut the eye. **Note:** If you are going to drill the holes for the star pattern, do not drill all the way through the board. After all, the star pattern only makes sense seen from one side. Make sure to use a small-diameter bit for the stars—these holes are only to mark where the stars go, not for actual mounting of a jewel or nail. That happens later.

2 This photo shows the complete pattern with all the holes drilled.

3 Start cutting at the hoof on the left front leg and continue the cut.

4 Continue the cut.

5 Cut around the left front leg and remove it. Peel the pattern off and set the piece aside.

6 Continue toward the head. Do the details as you go. If you do, you won't have to cut them holding on to a very small piece.

7 Face cut. As before, detail as you go. It's easier to hold on to a board foot than a board inch.

8 Notice the position of the hands when preparing to make a sharp turn.

9 Insert the blade to cut the eye. It is important to do this before you cut the face free.

10 Notice the position of the hands when preparing to make a sharp turn. The hand in front holds the puzzle steady while the back hand swings the material through the cut.

11 In addition to setting each piece aside as I cut it free, I assemble the puzzle. I also make sure the pieces slide easily in and out from both directions. If I find I am having trouble sliding the pieces in and out, I can change blades or make any needed adjustments to my saw as I go.

12 There are four pieces left to cut.

13 Hold tight! Don't lose concentration while cutting the last few pieces.

14 I've always wondered what I could do with all those negative spaces. In this case, I will use the carrier to keep from crunching the puzzle when running it through the drum sander.

15 He is a good-looking old goat.

Section 2: Sanding

There are two reasons to sand your puzzle (or any other project). The first is to correct mistakes in cutting. With puzzles, the most common problem is that the pieces stick. This is remedied by careful sanding of the head of the key and of the shoulders of the keyhole. Sand lightly and test the fit. It's easy to overdo it.

The second reason to sand is to improve the surfaces of your puzzle. I do a three-step sanding process: 1) sand the top and bottom of each piece, 2) check the cut surfaces for smoothness and gently touch up any rough spots, and 3) round over all of the edges. The three-step process gives a professional finish to each puzzle.

Occasionally, I find I have cut a puzzle that won't stand. This means the bottom is not flat. In such cases, I use my disc sander with a 90° table. I hold the base against the moving disc.

I like to sand the top and bottom of each puzzle using my drum sander. To keep the puzzle from shifting sideways or twisting under the drum, I use one or two push sticks to support the puzzle as it goes through. If you have a drum sander, see the tip box below for more information.

Using a drum sander

I find that using a drum sander has cut my sanding time by 60%. If you have a relatively good surface to begin with, you can sand with only a finish grit. I usually use a 220- or 180-grit belt.

Note: There are puzzles that I cannot put through the drum sander without breaking them. I've placed a "drum sander" symbol (**O**) on the patterns that can be sanded with the drum sander. You can use a drum sander on all of the patterns, provided that you save the scrap and use it as a carrier. The patterns marked with the **O** symbol go through with only a rubber band around them.

To use a drum sander to sand your puzzles, follow the steps below:

- Put a rubber band completely around the outside of each puzzle. Rubber band size #64 works for most of the puzzles in this book.
- If you're doing several puzzles, group them by how thick the wood is.
- Start with the group made of the thickest wood.
- Position each puzzle on the conveyor belt so that it goes through with the grain (otherwise the drum will leave visible marks).
- Run the first group through on both sides. Use one or more push sticks to support each puzzle as it goes through.
- Adjust the height of the sanding drum for the next group.

You'll have to experiment with this process. Start with some of the simpler puzzles to get the hang of it.

Another option to sand the top and bottom of the puzzle, if you don't have a drum sander, is to use a disc sanding pad chucked in a drill secured by a stand (see box below) or a sanding block.

After sanding the top and bottom of each puzzle piece, I check the cut surfaces for smoothness. Any part that someone is likely to touch should be smooth. Gently touch up any rough places to keep the fit. I prefer to use a disc sanding pad chucked in a drill secured by a stand (see box below), but you could also use sandpaper wrapped around a dowel.

My last step is to round over all of the edges. Rounding over the edges gives a nice finish, provides visual separation of the pieces, and sometimes removes a flaw. I use a Sand-O-Flex flap sander with 240-grit scored refill and cut along the scored lines. I end up with 64 ⅛" (3mm) strips of sandpaper. You can adjust the length of the strips for larger and smaller pieces. While you are using the Sand-O-Flex, I recommend you use rubber finger protectors, which are available at office supply stores. I prefer to mount the Sand-O-Flex on a drill secured in a drill stand (see box below), but you can also use a drill press, as shown here.

A flex drum sander, such as the one offered by Guinevere Sanding System, can be used instead of a Sand-O-Flex to round over some of the edges of a puzzle piece. It can also be used to sand some of the cut surfaces of a piece. However, it may be too large to reach all of the small places on the puzzle pieces in this book.

Sanding Techniques

In place of a drum sander, you can use a 5" (127mm) disc sanding pad (220 grit) chucked into a drill secured by a drill stand or a drill press. Before we invested in the drum sander, I used to do all of my flat sanding this way. Just be careful to keep the flat sides level as you sand and wear finger protection. The only problem I've had using the disc sander in this way is occasionally sanding a piece unevenly. You will improve with practice. You can also use the Sand-O-Flex in this way.

Section 3: Finishing

Because I usually want the actual wood colors to come through, I use natural-colored Danish oil to finish my puzzles. I've had good luck with the General Finishes brand.

The color of most woods will change over time because of exposure to ultraviolet rays. If you want the color to hold, use a clear, UV-blocking Danish oil on the wood. The tech person I spoke to at General Finishes said their product doubles the life of the color. General Finishes sells this product under the name "Outdoor Oil." Personally, since I last recommended this product in *Animal Puzzles for the Scroll Saw*, I've stopped using it. The pieces needed more rubbing than I have time for (or my customers want to pay for).

Because making and selling puzzles is my business, I do a lot of oiling. I start by pouring the oil into a one-gallon, resealable freezer bag. Next, I disassemble the puzzle and drop the pieces into the oil. I let them sit in the oil for a short time. I remove them from the bag and place them on plastic trays lined with paper towels to drip dry.

Most of the pieces dry completely without wiping, but I inspect all of the pieces and wipe as necessary. The more cut line detail there is in a puzzle piece, the more attention it needs at this step. This is because more oil gets into the cut line than can be absorbed by the surfaces internal to any given cut. Then it bleeds out, usually over several hours.

After drying the pieces that need it, I reassemble the puzzle and let it air-dry overnight. Remember, oil fumes are extremely volatile. I dry the pieces with paper towels, because they dry quickly and completely. I dispose of the paper towels by dropping them loosely into a large paper bag and letting them dry overnight. Doing so prevents a buildup of fumes that could spontaneously combust. The important thing is not to stuff oil-soaked rags into an airtight container.

Section 4: Marking the constellation

Tools and Materials

- Drill press
- Silver wire (14 and/or 18 gauge), crystal jewels, or stainless steel finishing nails
- Wire cutters
- Sanding method of choice
- Gap-filling cyanoacrylate
- Toothpick
- Small hammer
- Needle-nose pliers or tweezers

Wiring

You can also insert silver wire into your puzzles. Snip pieces of the wire to about 3/8" (10mm). To drill the entry holes, use a drill bit that matches the wire gauge and drill holes a little short of 3/8" (10mm). Insert a wire piece and tap into place using a small hammer. No glue is necessary if your wire and drill bit are the same diameter and you tap the wire in about a millimeter. If your wire is too long, it will bend over—silver wires are too soft to pound like a nail. If you've accidentally drilled the hole for the wire too large, flatten the top of the wire to cover the gap by hammering it a bit more.

Jewelling

A third sparkly choice is showing the stars with small crystal jewels available at craft stores. Mount a teardrop-shaped bit in your drill press or rotary power tool. Drill the gem holes to the depth of the gems you have. (This will vary considerably depending on the effect you want.) If using a rotary tool, you can drill by hand or with a small brace. It's easier to judge depth and diameter with the brace, but I found it took too long. Using a drill press eliminates this problem.

Use clear glue such as gap-filling cyanoacrylate. Put a tiny drop of glue in the hole with a toothpick and carefully place the gem. Needle-nose pliers or tweezers make this easier. Clean off any excess glue and admire your work.

Jewelling is best done after your piece has been oiled and dried. When you drill the gem hole, you will go down to bare wood, so the glue will stick better.

Finishing nails

1 You've already drilled shallow holes to show the placement of the stars. The next step is to mount a small stainless steel finishing nail in your drill press. Be sure to use stainless steel nails, or the moisture content of the wood and the solvents in the Danish oil finish may cause rust or discoloration. Holding the puzzle piece firmly, turn on the drill press and push the nail most of the way into the wood. Use wire cutters to snip off the nail as close to the wood as possible.

2 After sanding the nail down to the level of the wood, you'll have a shiny star marking a place in the constellation.

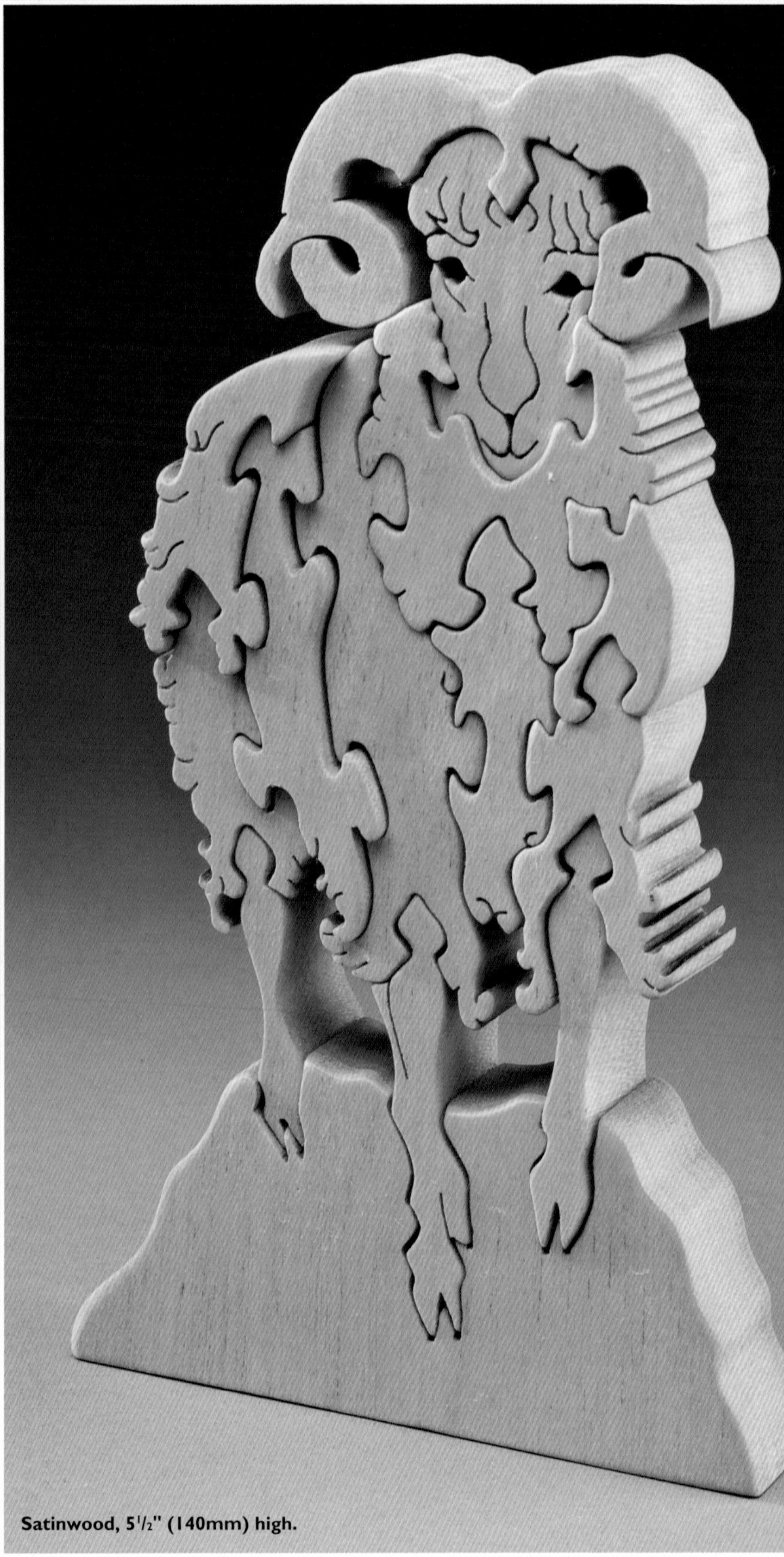

Satinwood, 5 1/2" (140mm) high.

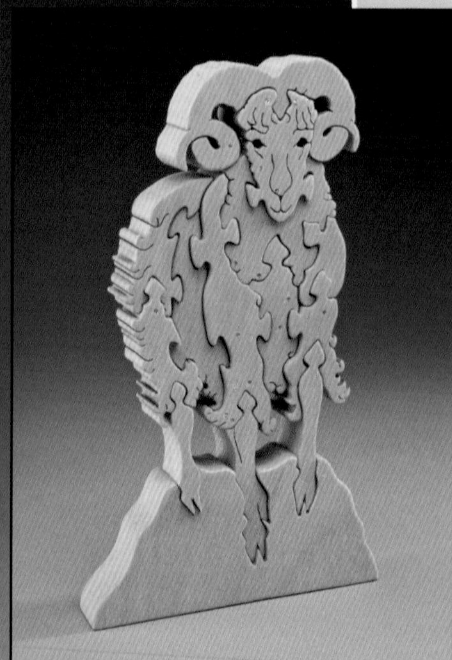

♈ Aries: the Ram

March 21–April 19

More than 2,000 years ago, the vernal equinox commonly occurred in Aries, so that is why it is the first sign of the zodiac. Hamal is the bright star in Aries' horn.

In mythology, the goddess Nephele sent a ram with Golden Fleece to save her children from being sacrificed. The ram carried the son to safety—the daughter fell off over the sea. When he arrived, the son sacrificed the ram and gave the Golden Fleece to King Aeetes. Jupiter placed the ram in the sky. Later, Jason and the Argonauts stole the fleece.

Aries are usually courageous, adventurous, and quick thinkers, though they can also be selfish, impatient, and impulsive.

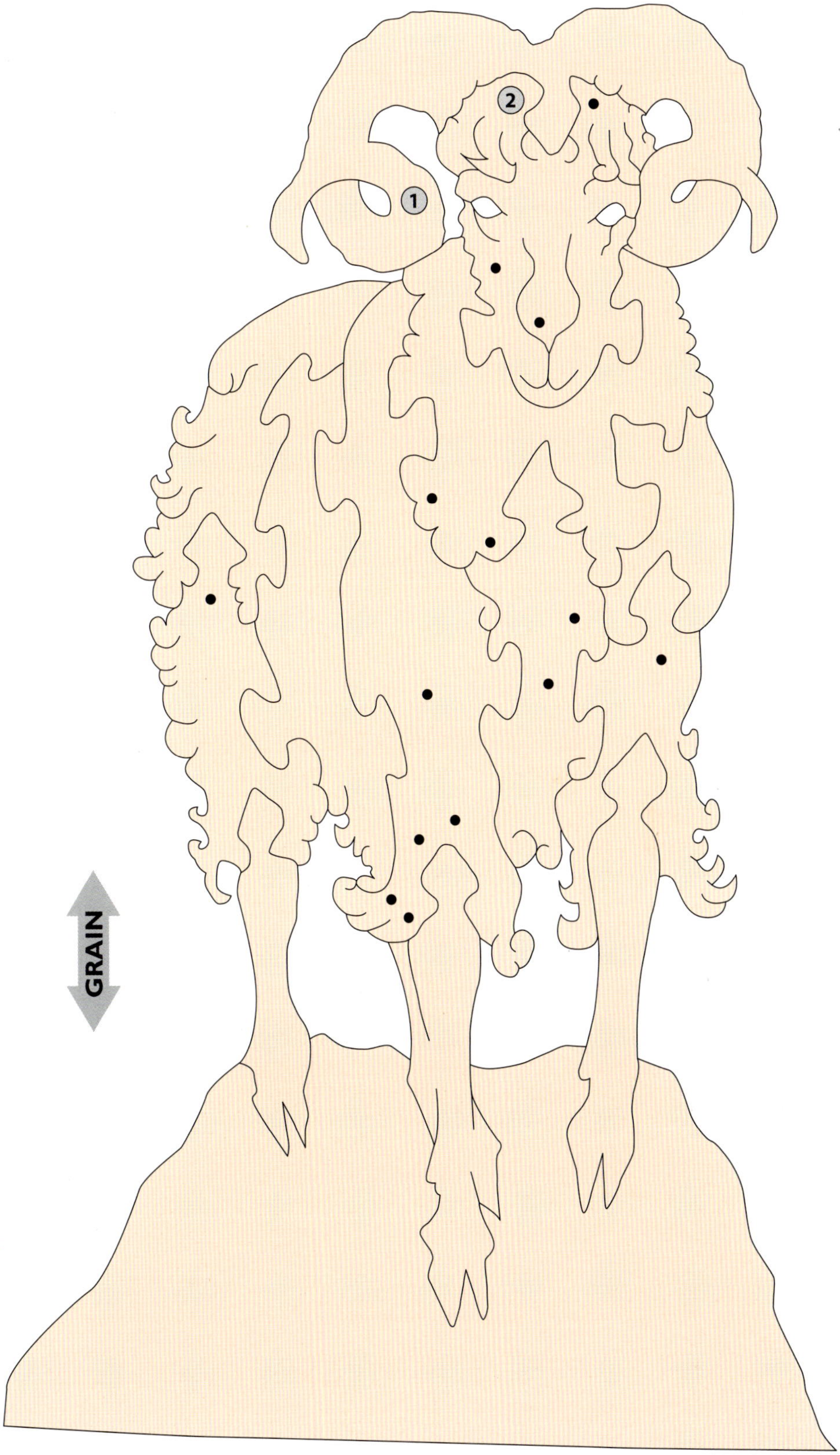

○ = major star
• = minor star

Star Name Key:
1. Hamal
2. Sheratan

Walnut, 7" (178mm) high.

♉ Taurus: the Bull

April 20–May 20

The bull has always been an important animal in Roman mythology. Bacchus, the wine god, chose the bull as his animal. Additionally, Jupiter turned himself into a white bull to seduce Europa. The orange eye of Taurus is Aldebaran, one of the brightest stars that can be seen from Earth. Two star clusters are present in the constellation—the Pleiades (the Seven Sisters), which can be viewed with the naked eye even in light polluted areas, and the Hyades, which form the closest open star cluster to Earth.

Tauri are usually patient, loving, and determined, though they can be possessive, inflexible, and self-indulgent.

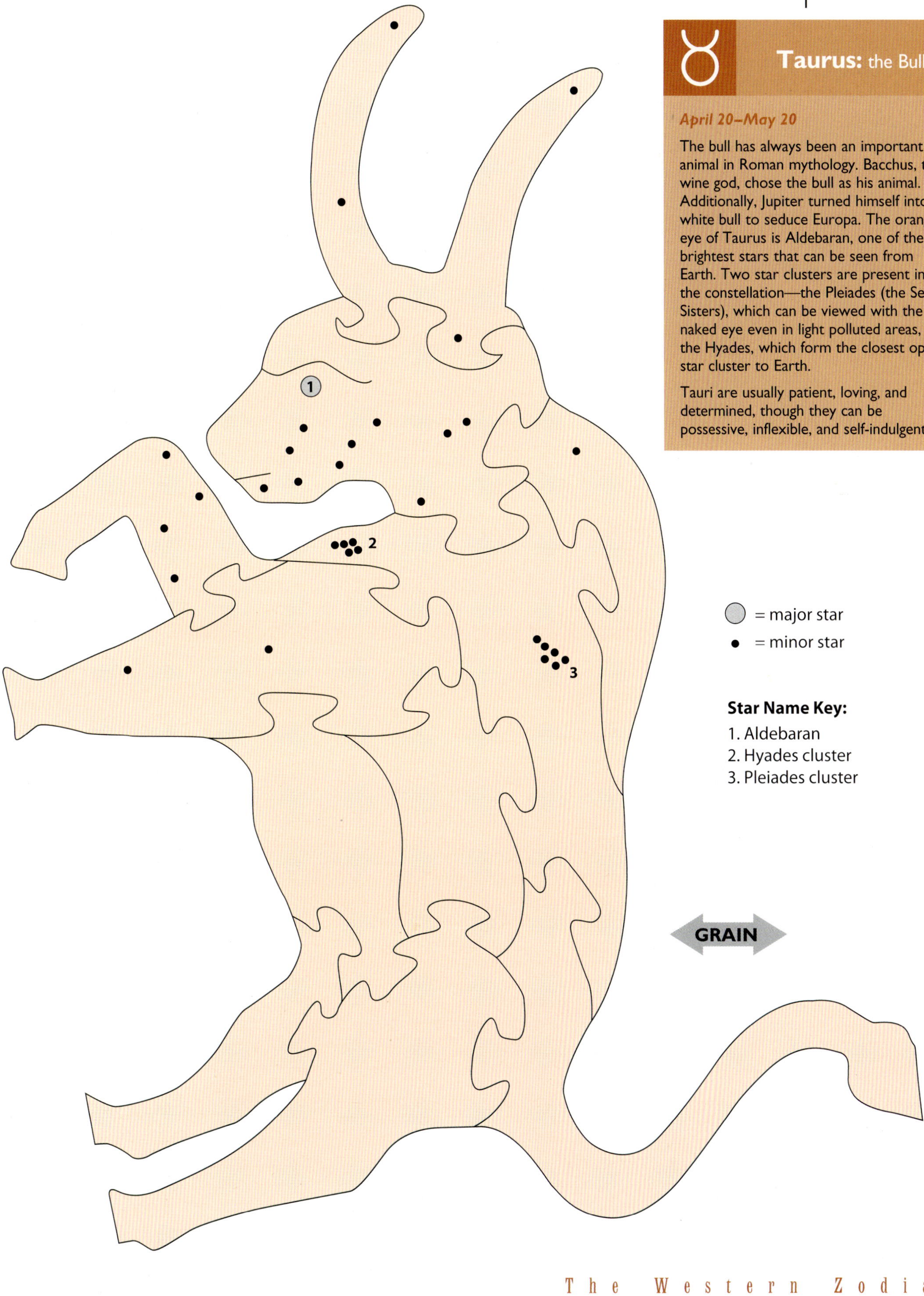

◯ = major star

● = minor star

Star Name Key:

1. Aldebaran
2. Hyades cluster
3. Pleiades cluster

The Western Zodiac — Easy Pattern

Mesquite, 7" (178mm) high.

II Gemini: the Twins

May 21–June 20

In mythology, Castor and Pollux were twins who sailed with Jason and the Argonauts. Though Pollux was immortal, Castor was not. When Castor was killed, Pollux was so heartbroken that Jupiter put them both in the sky. The two bright stars in the constellation are actually named Castor and Pollux.

Geminis are usually versatile, lively, good communicators, though they can be tense, inconsistent, and cunning.

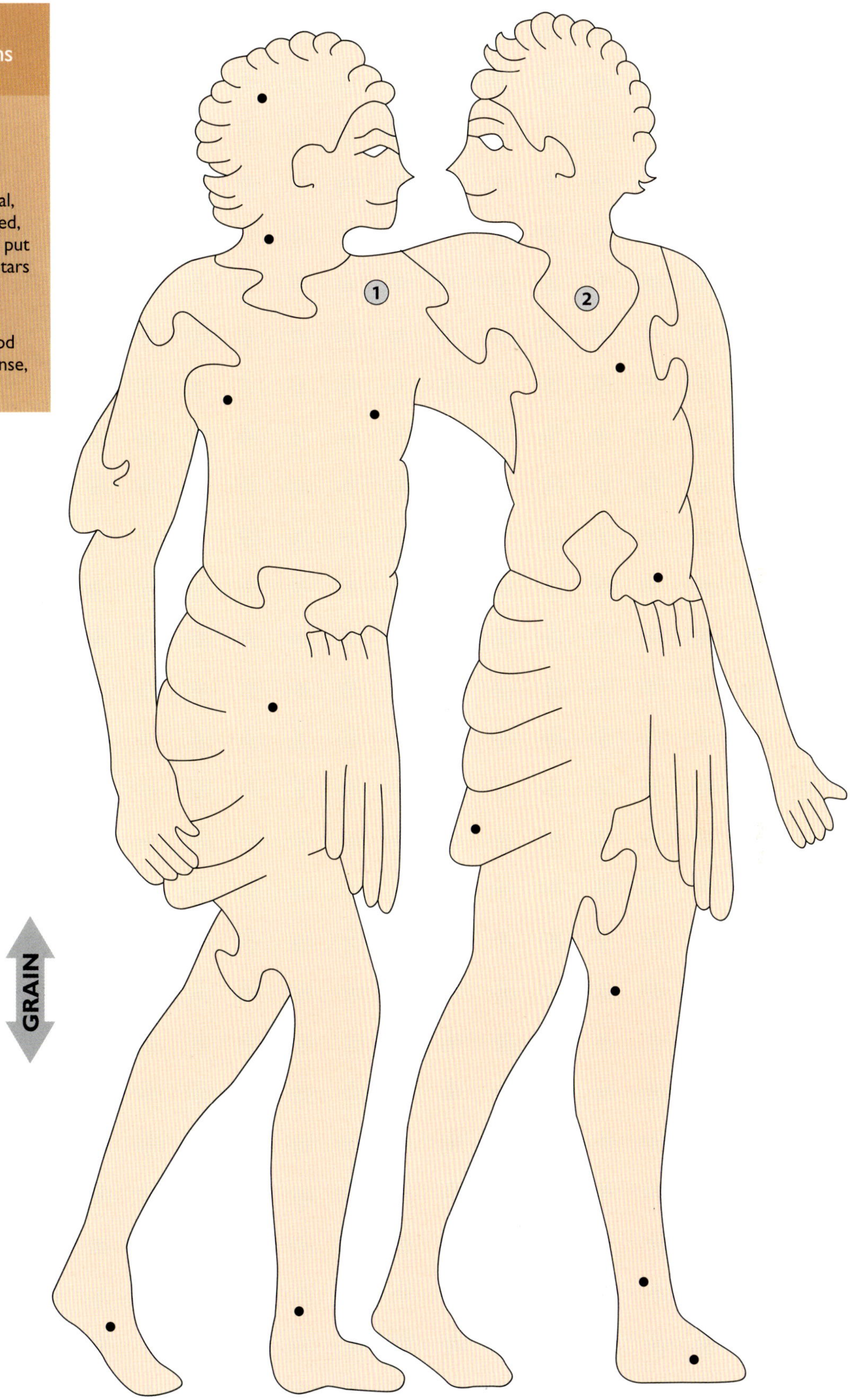

◯ = major star

• = minor star

Star Name Key:

1. Pollux
2. Castor

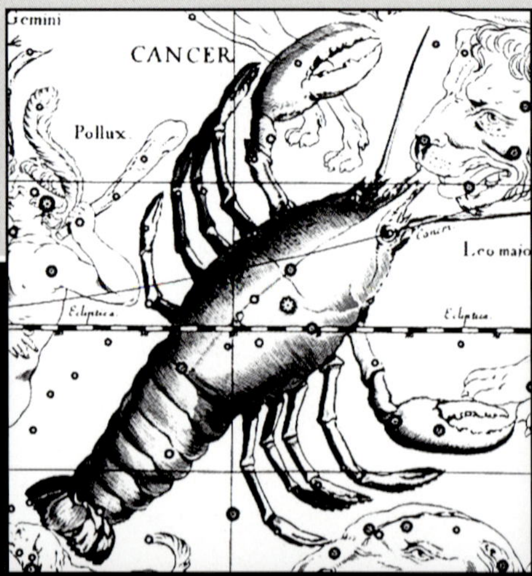

Zebrawood, 6½" (165mm) high.

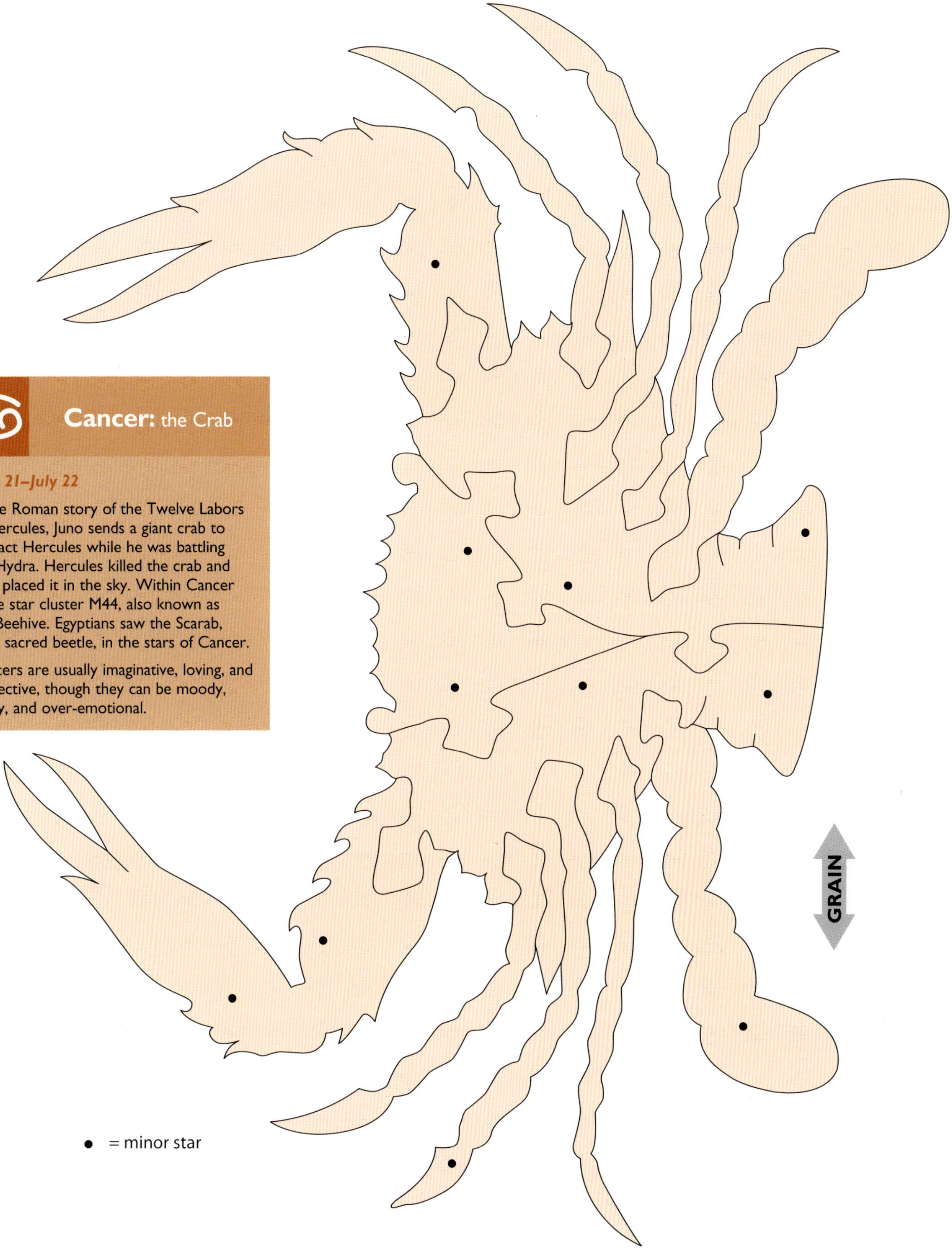

♋ Cancer: the Crab

June 21–July 22

In the Roman story of the Twelve Labors of Hercules, Juno sends a giant crab to distract Hercules while he was battling the Hydra. Hercules killed the crab and Juno placed it in the sky. Within Cancer is the star cluster M44, also known as the Beehive. Egyptians saw the Scarab, their sacred beetle, in the stars of Cancer.

Cancers are usually imaginative, loving, and protective, though they can be moody, clingy, and over-emotional.

● = minor star

Osage-orange, 4" (101mm) high.

♌ Leo: the Lion

July 23–August 22

The myth of Hercules tells of the Nemean Lion, which had an impenetrable skin. Hercules killed the lion and it was placed in the sky as a tribute to his victory. Leo is one of the easiest constellations to find—just look for the backward question mark in Leo's head. Regulus, the star at his front hip (and the point of the question mark), is one of the brightest stars in the sky. The Leonid meteor shower comes from this direction every November.

Leos are usually generous, creative, and faithful, though they can be patronizing, bossy, and intolerant.

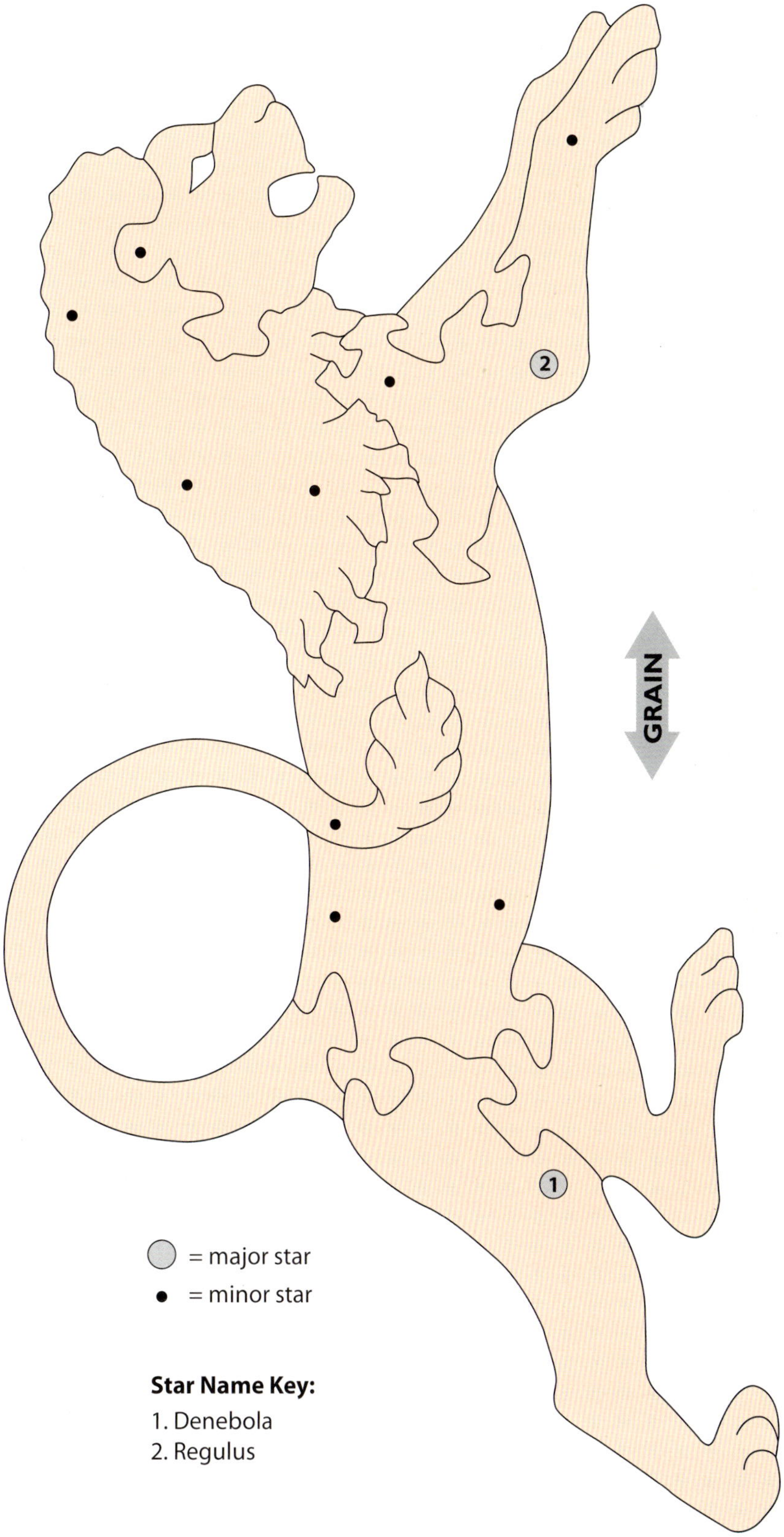

○ = major star

• = minor star

Star Name Key:

1. Denebola
2. Regulus

Birch, 8" (203mm) high.

♍ Virgo: the Virgin

August 23–September 22

Virgo has been identified as many different women, from Ceres to the Virgin Mary. Ceres was the Roman goddess of the fields, who had a beautiful daughter named Proserpina. One day, Pluto saw Proserpina and stole her away to be his wife. The distraught Ceres stopped tending the crops, and this is what caused the first autumn and winter. Jupiter determined Proserpina should be allowed to spend six months of the year with her mother—thus causing the renewal of spring and summer. Fittingly, the constellation appears only during the spring and summer, and hides during the last half of the year. Spica, the star in the wheat sheaf Virgo carries, is one of the brightest stars in the sky, and is used by sailors to navigate.

Virgos are usually modest, reliable, and intelligent, though they can be critical perfectionists and worriers.

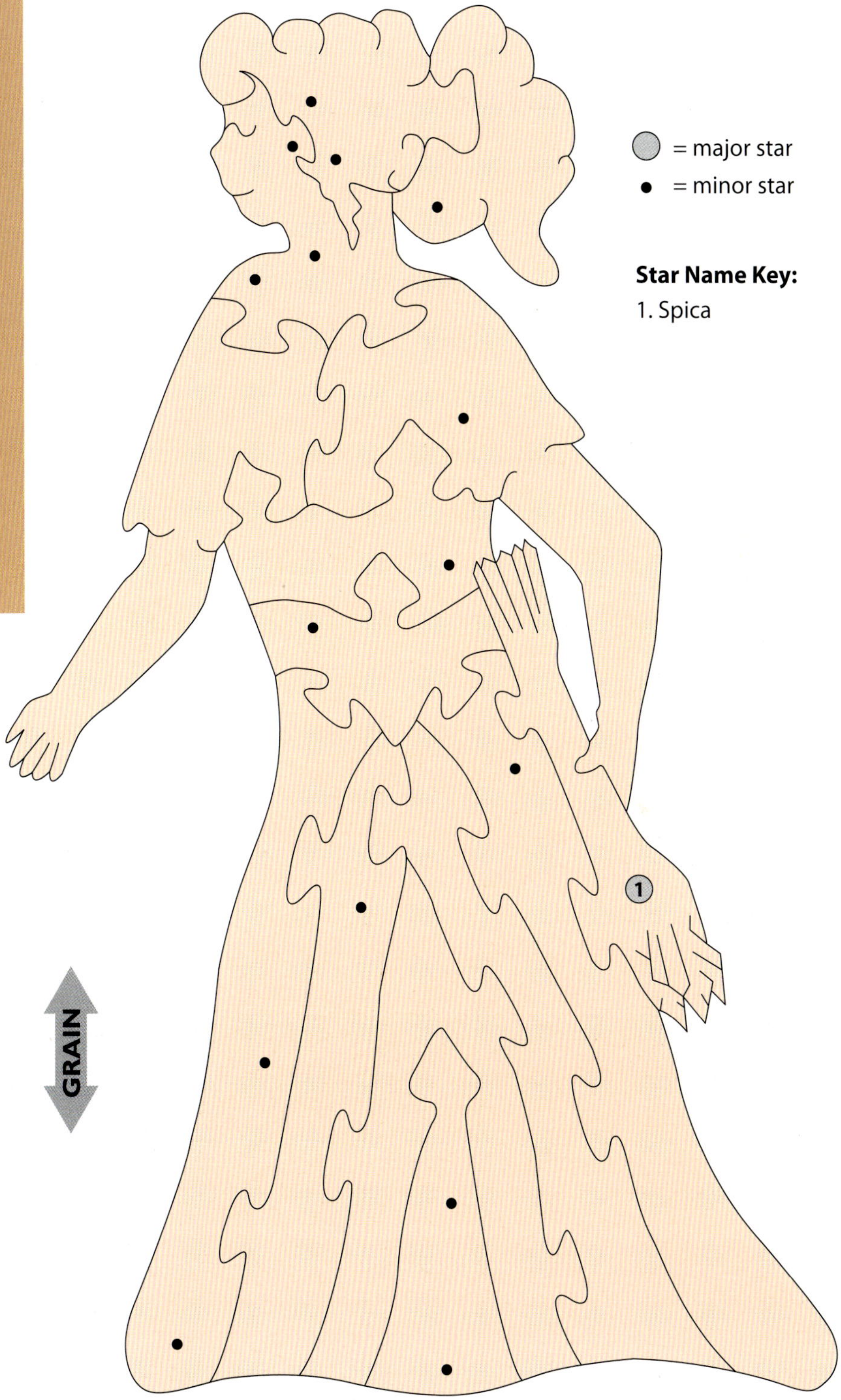

○ = major star

● = minor star

Star Name Key:

1. Spica

Macacaubo, 7½" (190mm) high.

Libra

Libra: the Scales

September 23–October 22

Libra used to rise during the fall equinox, when the day and night are equal. Originally, the two brightest stars of Libra—Zubenelgenubi and Zubeneschamali—were the claws of Scorpio.

Librans are usually diplomatic, charming, and sociable, though they can be indecisive, easily influenced, and self-indulgent.

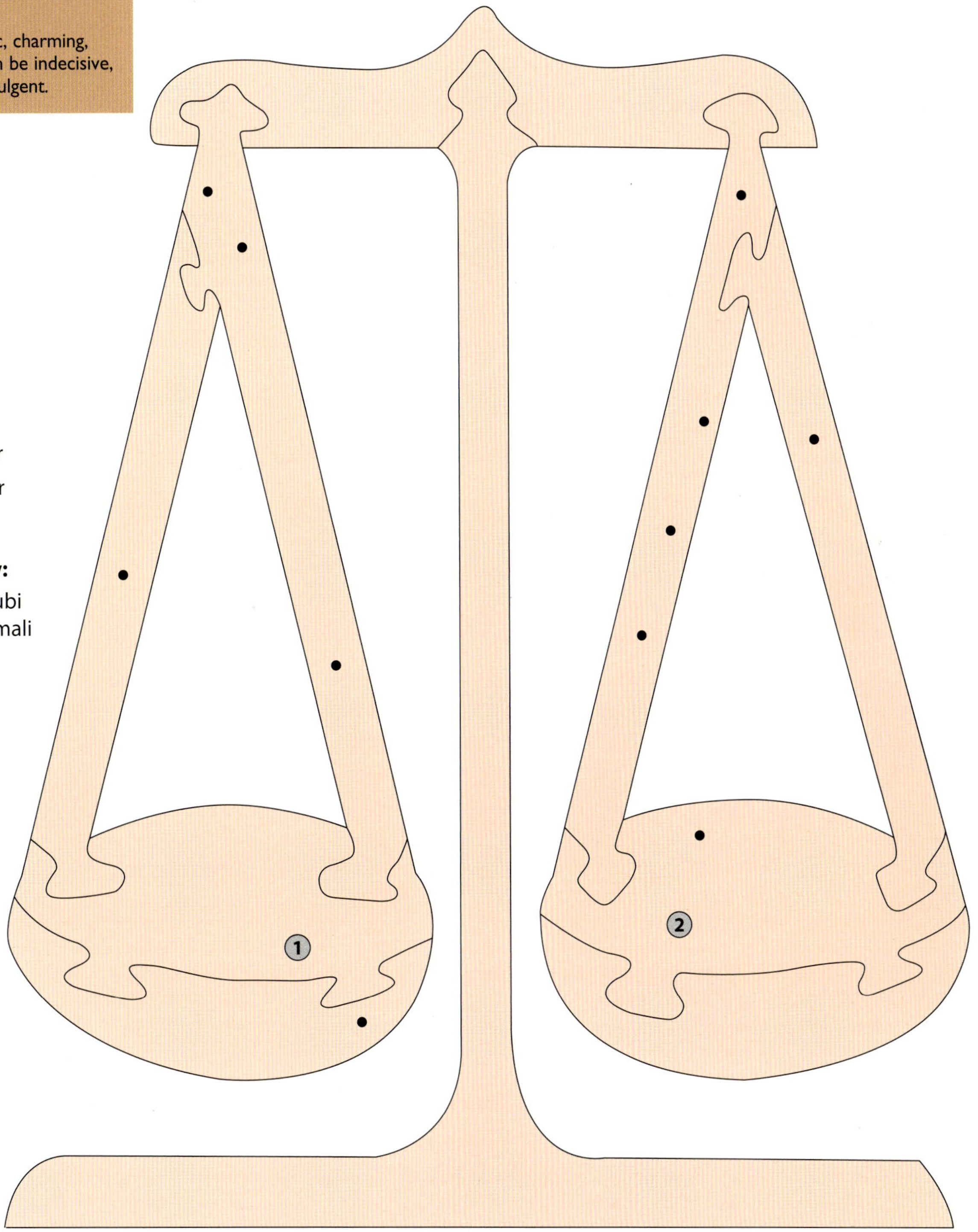

○ = major star
• = minor star

Star Name Key:

1. Zubenelgenubi
2. Zubeneschamali

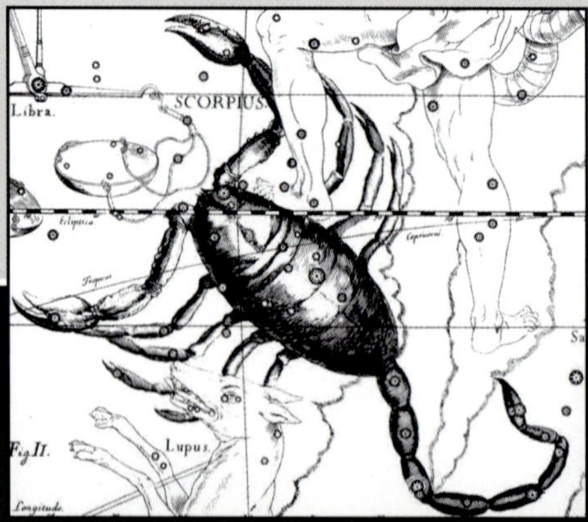

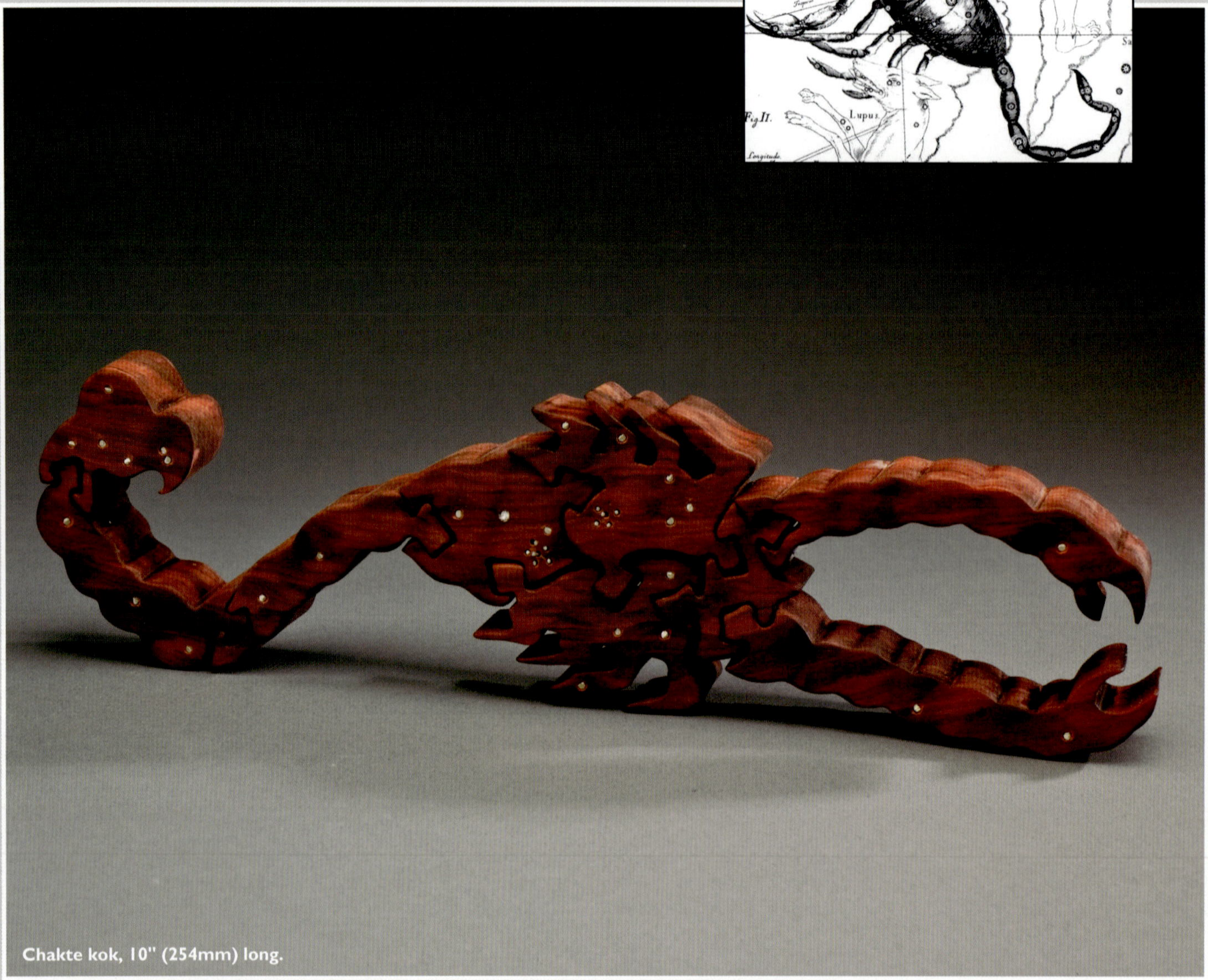

Chakte kok, 10" (254mm) long.

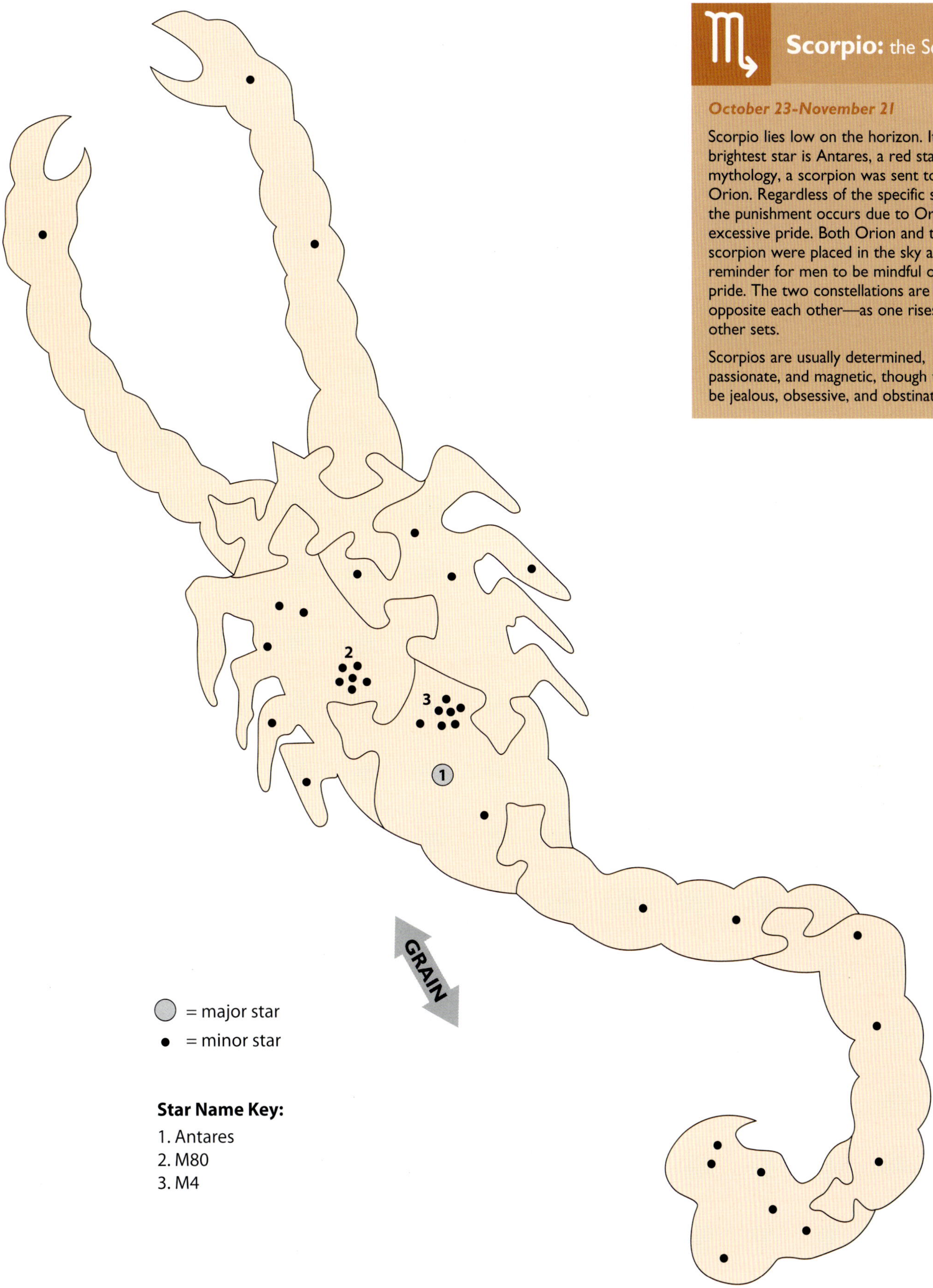

♏ Scorpio: the Scorpion

October 23-November 21

Scorpio lies low on the horizon. Its brightest star is Antares, a red star. In mythology, a scorpion was sent to kill Orion. Regardless of the specific story, the punishment occurs due to Orion's excessive pride. Both Orion and the scorpion were placed in the sky as a reminder for men to be mindful of their pride. The two constellations are always opposite each other—as one rises, the other sets.

Scorpios are usually determined, passionate, and magnetic, though they can be jealous, obsessive, and obstinate.

○ = major star
● = minor star

Star Name Key:

1. Antares
2. M80
3. M4

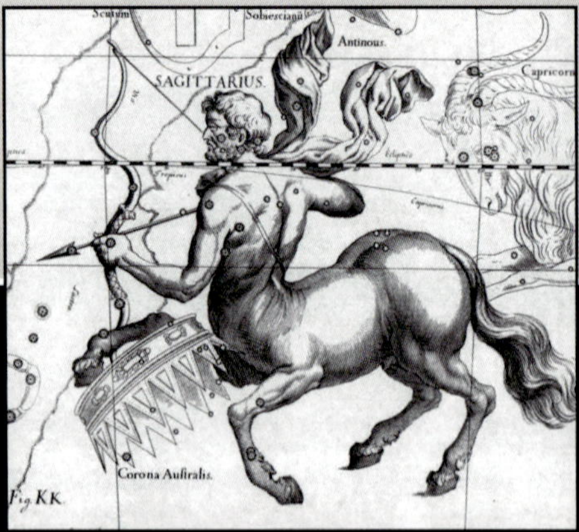

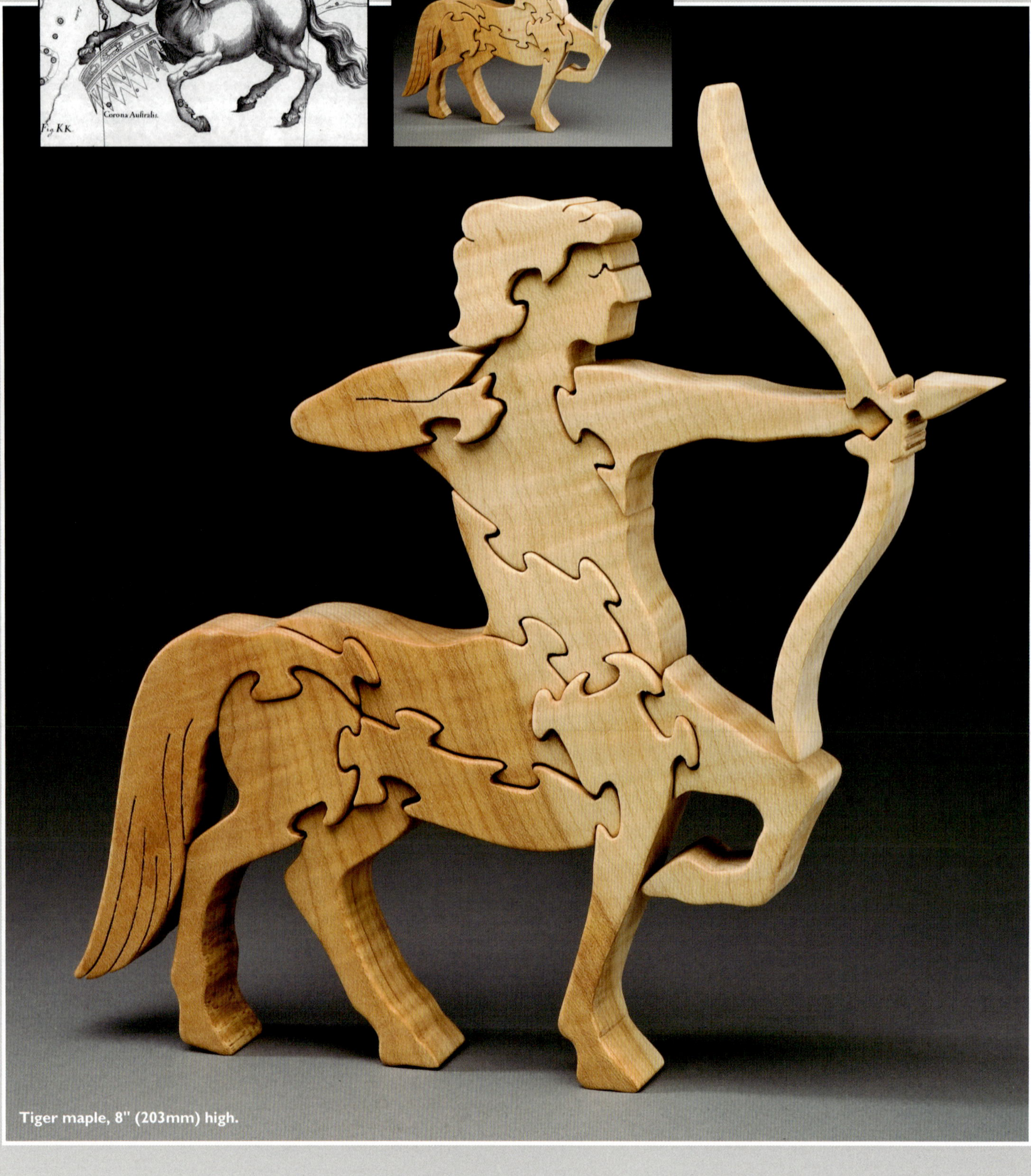

Tiger maple, 8" (203mm) high.

Sagittarius:
the Centaur Archer

November 22–December 21

Crotus, the son of the nymph Eupheme and the god Pan, lived with the Muses and was known in Greek mythology to have invented the bow. The Muses requested that he be immortalized in the sky, and Sagittarius was formed. My long-time favorite author, Anne McCaffrey, placed her dragon planet, Pern, around "Rukbat in the Sagittarian sector." The Swan or Omega Nebula is also located within Sagittarius.

Sagittarians are usually optimistic, good-humored, and intelligent, though they can be careless, irresponsible, and tactless.

○ = major star
● = minor star

Star Name Key:
1. Rukbat
2. Nunki

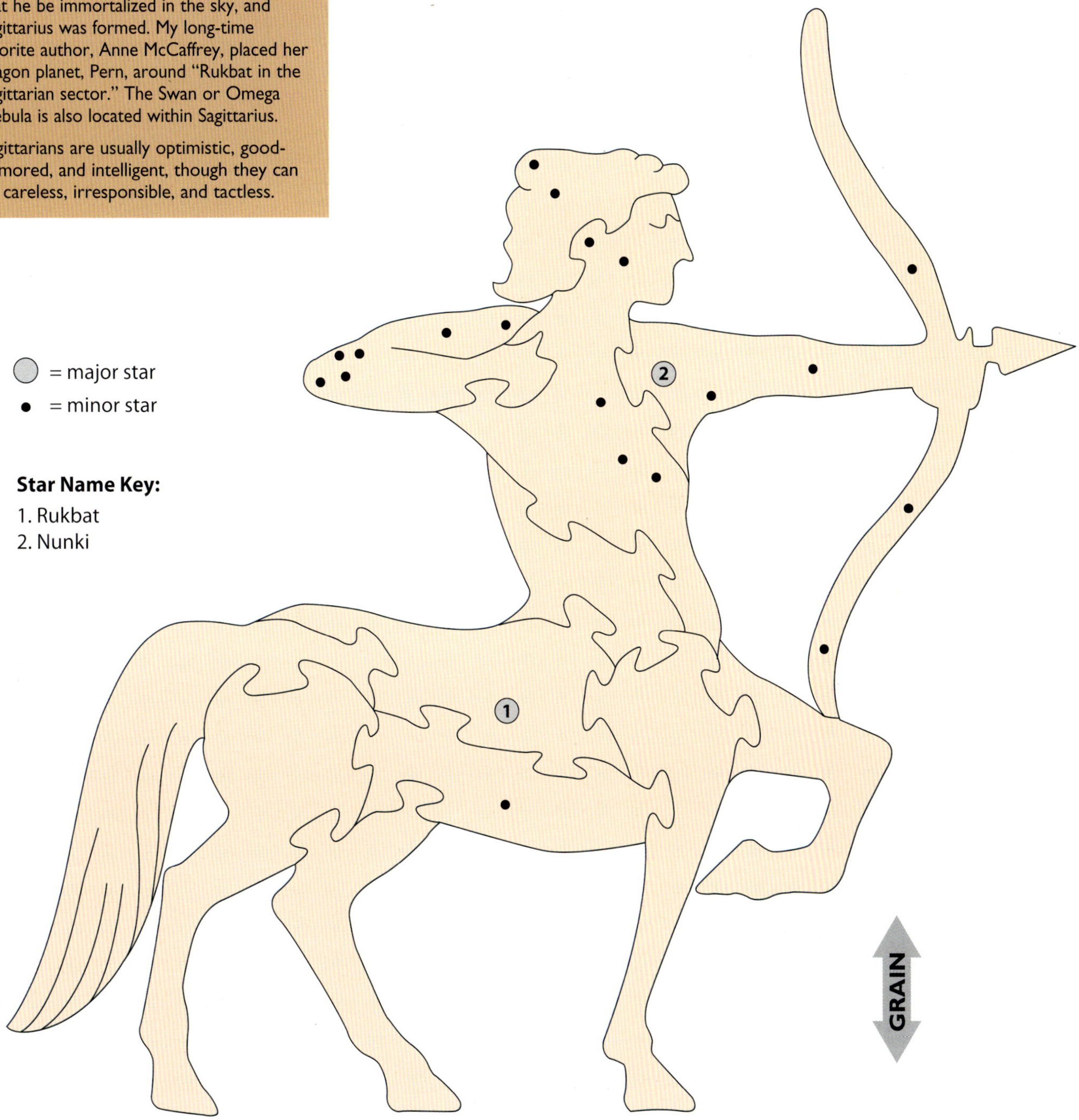

Enlarge pattern at 134%.

The Western Zodiac — Easy Pattern

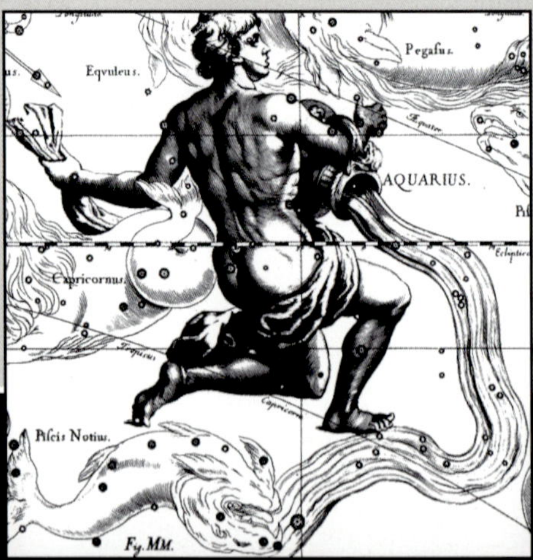

Sycamore, 7" (178mm) high.

Aquarius: the Water Carrier

January 20–February 18

Water carriers and cupbearers were important during classical times. In Roman mythology, Ganymede was the water carrier for Jupiter and accompanied the god everywhere. Ganymede was also believed to have caused the great flood.

Aquarians are usually friendly, honest, and independent, though they can be unpredictable, detached, and contrary.

◯ = major star

● = minor star

Star Name Key:

1. Sadalsuud
2. Sadalmelik
3. Scheat
4. Fomolhaut

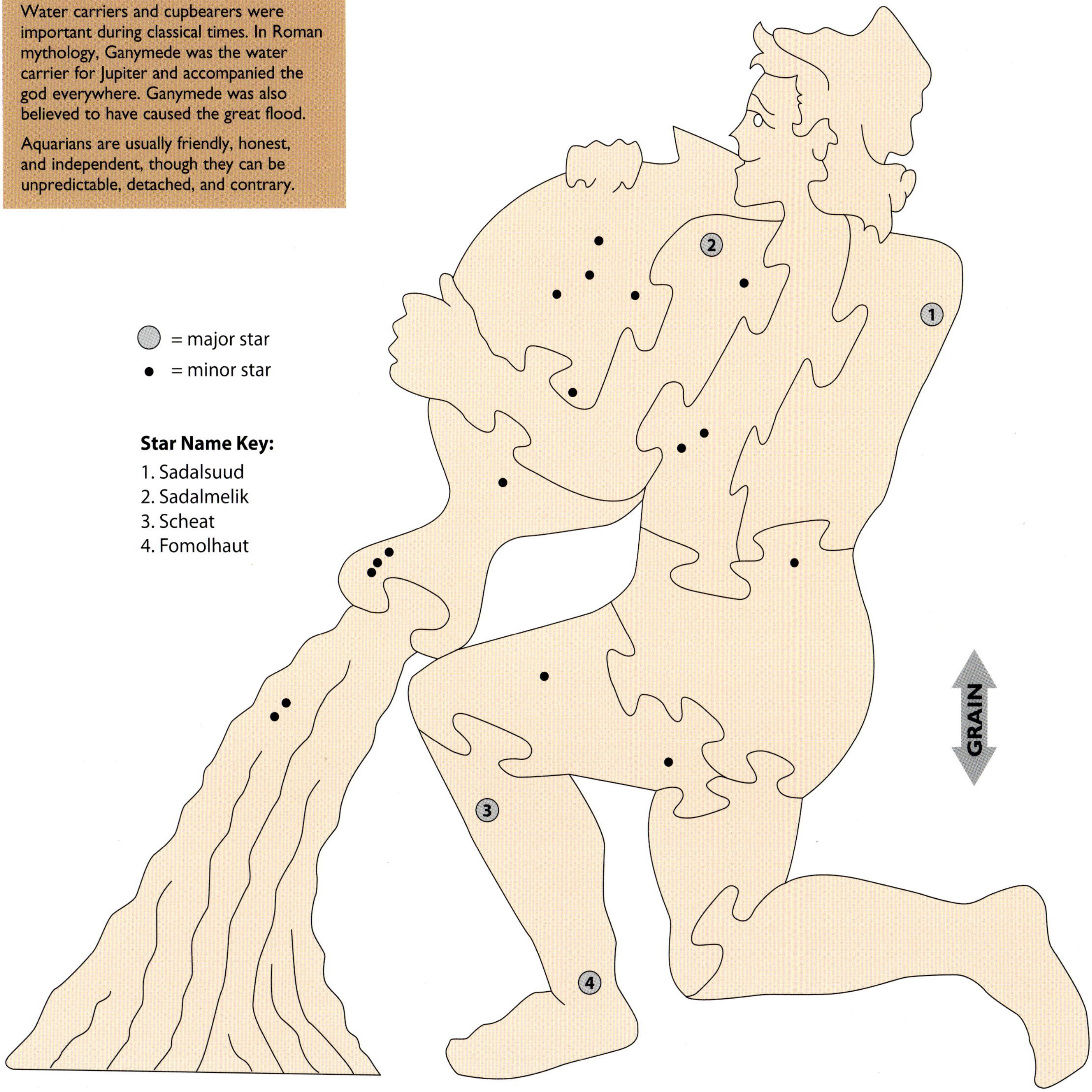

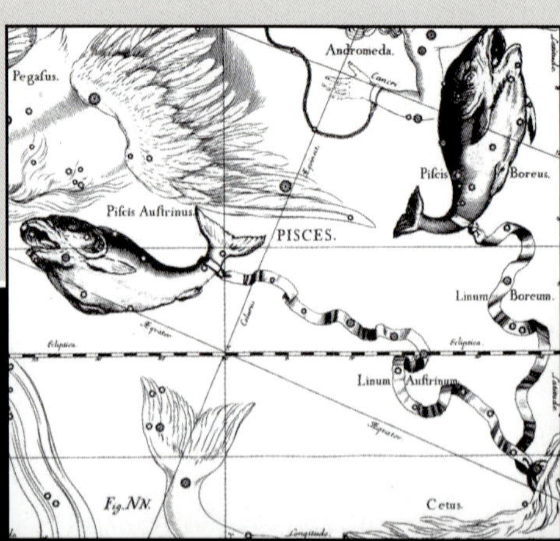

Mesquite, 6" (152mm) high.

Pisces: the Fish

February 19–March 20

The two fish of Pisces are said to represent Venus and Cupid, her son. When attacked by Typhon the monster (the same incident that Capricorn immortalizes), they escaped by turning themselves into fishes. But in order not to lose each other in the murky water, they tied themselves together with a long rope. This is a constellation of inconspicuous stars, making it hard to find.

Pisces are usually imaginative, kind, and sympathetic, though they can be vague, secretive, and gullible.

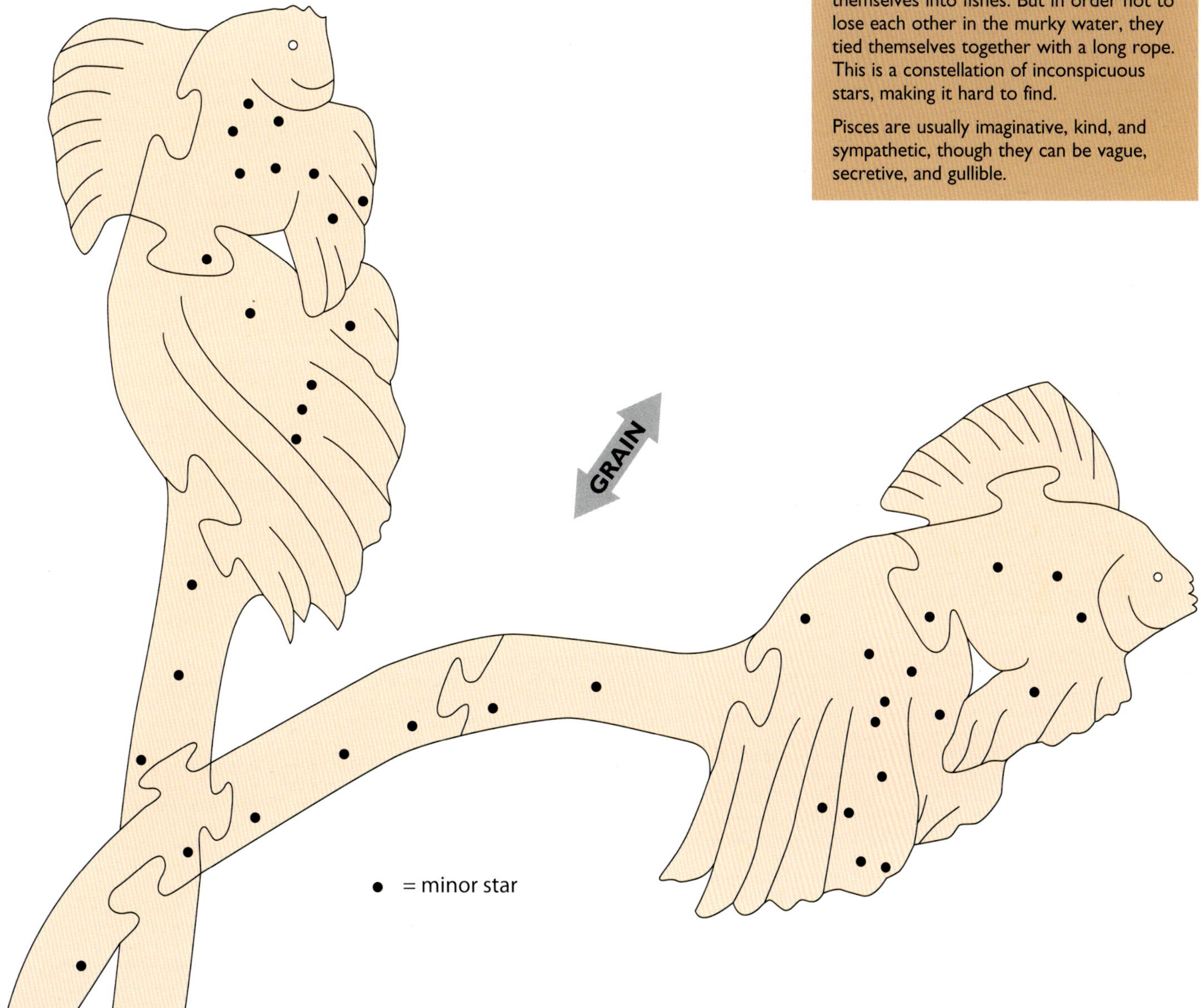

2 The Eastern Zodiac

The Western zodiac is based roughly on the months of the year. Characteristics are thought to be associated with those people born during any given period of time. The Chinese, or Eastern, zodiac takes a different approach; characteristics are assigned to people depending roughly on the year in which they were born. These animals do not have constellations.

There are several versions of the origin of the Chinese zodiac cycle. One involves a race of all the animals to the bedside of the Buddha—each of the twelve that arrived first had a year named after him. Another version involves a contest staged by the Jade Emperor for the most beautiful, cleverest, etc. Each of the winners had a year named after him.

The basic twelve-year cycle is also part of a larger 60-year cycle. The 60-year cycle is based on the twelve animals plus a rotation of the five elements: water, wood, fire, metal, and earth. This results in combinations with even more specific personality characteristics, such as a wood ox or a water dragon. In addition, the two primal forces, yin (odd years) and yang (even years), influence the positive and negative sides of the various combinations of animal and elemental signs. And you thought the Western zodiac was complicated!

To find out what sign under which you were born, consult the chart on page 94.

Because the Eastern zodiac rotates according to the lunar cycle—not the solar, like Western years—the Chinese New Year is not synchronized with January 1. If you were born late in January or early in February, your sign is probably associated with the prior year.

Each puzzle includes more than just a pattern and photo of the completed project. The common Chinese symbol for each year is given, along with the years associated with the sign and a brief description of each personality. We've also included the inspiration for each puzzle pattern—a Chinese brush painting by artists Kimberly and Charlotte Fung Miller.

The Eastern Zodiac — Intermediate Pattern

Baltic birch, 13" (330mm) high.

Painting by Charlotte Fung Miller and Kimberly Sau Wai Miller.

马 Year of the Horse

People born in the Year of the Horse are sociable, hard-working, friendly, and tend to be popular. On the down side, they tend to be impatient and short-tempered. Horses get along with tigers and dogs, but not with rats.

Note: The step-by-step photos in this section were taken at the Fox Chapel Publishing studio. Dan Clarke painted the puzzle, and Scott Kriner photographed.

Setup

As I said earlier, Charlotte Fung Miller's painting of the Year of the Horse is partly responsible for the existence of this book. In thinking what to do with it (from a puzzle perspective), I decided to turn it into a frame tray puzzle. Because I thought it would look good, I adapted the background originally found in the Year of the Monkey painting into this puzzle.

I used 1/4" (6mm) Baltic birch for this project. It's good on both sides (no flaws), all the plies are birch (there is no softwood core), and it doesn't have voids (holes in the interior plies). Another advantage of Baltic birch is its light color, which makes it suitable for painting.

Because the cutting of this puzzle is similar to the Capricorn step-by-step, I'll be concentrating on the creation of the tray and the painting of the puzzle.

Enlarge pattern at 133%.

Make the frame tray puzzle

1 Choose two boards of about the same size. One will be the frame and the puzzle; the other will be the backer.

2 Glue the puzzle pattern on the top piece. Be sure to allow extra to make the frame. Drill an access hole and cut the frame free.

3 Sand both sides of the backer board. Glue the frame to the backer and clamp overnight.

4 Use the scroll saw to trim the outside of the glued backer and frame, then sand and round over the frame edges. Put the frame off to the side.

5 Drill the holes for the eye and nostrils in piece CC. Drill the nostril and eye holes in piece D.

6 Start cutting the puzzle pieces from one corner, and replace them in the frame as you cut each free. It's much easier to keep track of them that way.

7 Finish sand with a palm sander. Blow the dust out with canned air.

Tools and Materials

- 2 Baltic birch boards (¼" [6mm] thick) of the appropriate size
- Palm sander
- Wood glue
- Canned air
- Clamps
- Watercolor crayons, such as Karat Aquareil by Staedtler
- Brown stain, such as Behlen's Nutmeg
- Stain reducer, such as Behlen's Reducer
- Cotton swabs
- Hobby knife, such as X-Acto

Painting

As my regular readers know, I normally avoid painting. Paint, after all, is an add-on finish–that is, if you dip the pieces into the paint or paint with a brush, the paint takes up the space that should exist between the pieces. Because of that, the pieces won't slide in and out easily, as they are supposed to do. However, I experimented with surface painting in the following step-by-step.

1 After you've cut and sanded the puzzle, it should be smooth, dust-free, and ready to paint.

2 Using a piece of cardboard, flip the puzzle over and label the pieces according to the pattern (previous page). Flip the puzzle back over when you've finished.

3 I chose to color the puzzle so that it matched the brush painting on page 46. Begin by dampening the white crayon and undercoating all the pieces that will be white or gray. This will be all lettered pieces except P, BB-EE, and JJ.

4 Dampen the black crayon and coat the pieces that are to be solid black. These are P, BB-EE, and JJ.

5 Shade with the black crayon where gray areas are desired.

6 Use a damp cotton swab to blend the gray areas.

7 Use greens and browns to shade the four trees. These are pieces 3, 4, 10, and 11.

8 Use blues and whites to shade the waterfall—pieces 14 and 25.

9 Use a hobby knife, such as X-Acto, to clean up the interior cuts where the crayon has filled in the cut. Alternately, use plastic-backed sandpaper, such as Testor's hobby sanding film, or dental floss.

10 Start with a pan of straight stain, such as Behlen's Nutmeg. Stain the following pieces: 12, 13, and 15-24. Pour out some of the stain and add some reducer, such as Behlen's. Stain the following pieces: 2, and 5-9. Pour out some more of the stain mixture and add even more reducer. Stain piece 1. This three-tiered staining method will create a foreground, mid-ground, and background to the puzzle. When the pieces are dry, finish the whole puzzle—including the frame—with clear Danish oil.

11 Allow the pieces to dry and reassemble them. Congratulations—you've completed the project!

The Eastern Zodiac — Intermediate Pattern

Painting by Charlotte Fung Miller and Kimberly Sau Wai Miller.

Goncalo alves, 6" (152mm) high.

鼠 Year of the Rat

Rats are usually ambitious, honest, charming, generous, and able to maintain self-control. However, rats can also be possessive, anxious, and opinionated. They are compatible with dragons and monkeys, but not horses or rabbits.

Painting by Charlotte Fung Miller and Kimberly Sau Wai Miller.

Koa, 5" (127mm) high.

牛 Year of the Ox

Oxen are usually patient, hard workers, good listeners, and outstanding parents. However, oxen can also be stubborn, overly critical, and sulky. They are compatible with roosters and snakes, but not rams.

Painting by Charlotte Fung Miller and Kimberly Sau Wai Miller.

Zebrawood, 4" (101mm) high.

虎 Year of the Tiger

Tigers are usually aggressive, fun, and considerate. However, tigers can also be short-tempered, moody, and reckless. They are compatible with horses and dogs, but not monkeys or goats.

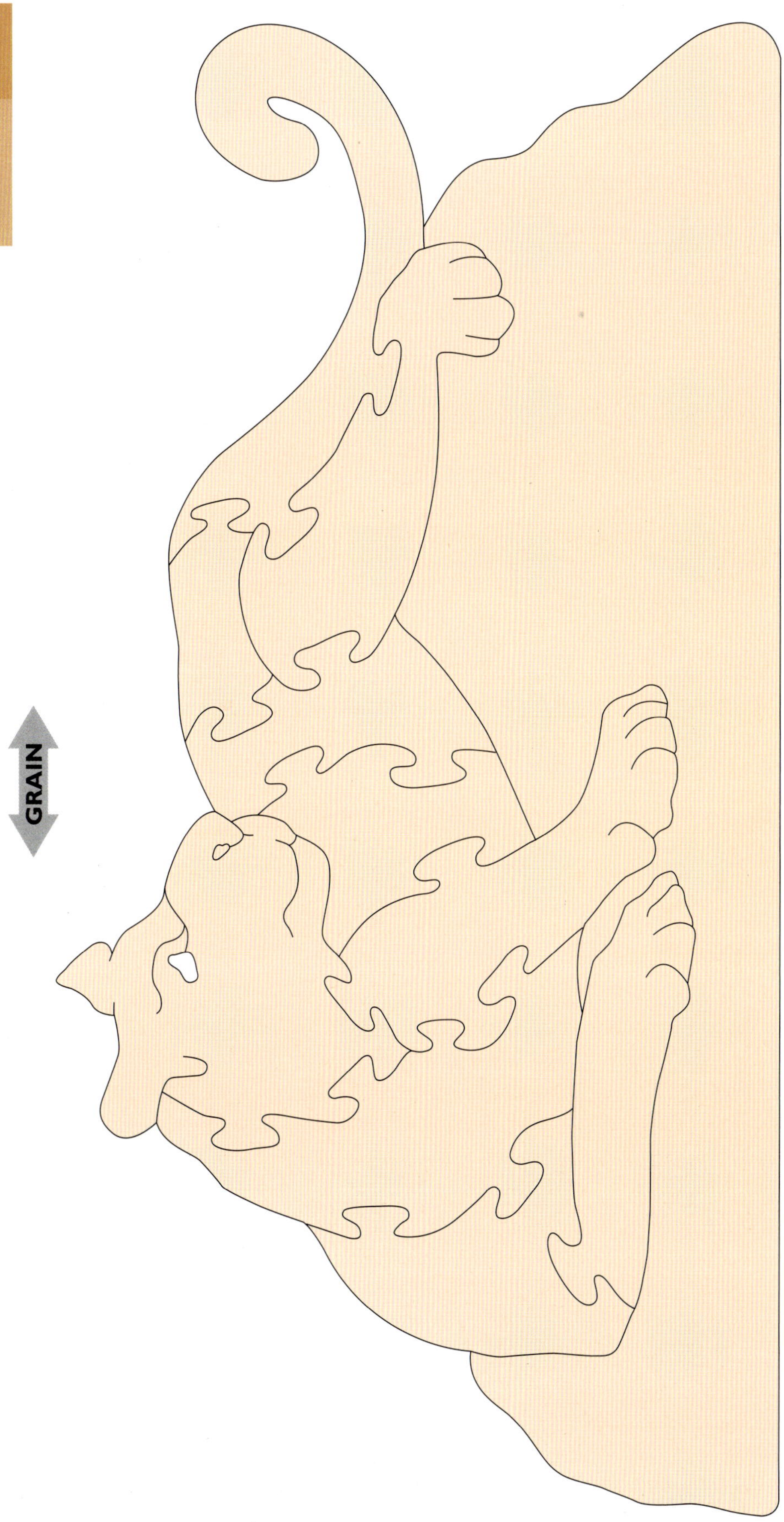

Painting by Charlotte Fung Miller and Kimberly Sau Wai Miller.

Aspen, $6^1/_2$" (165mm) high.

兔 Year of the Rabbit

Rabbits are usually talented, affectionate, and modest. However, rabbits can also be secretive, self-indulgent, and shy. They are compatible with rams and pigs, but not roosters.

The Eastern Zodiac – Advanced Pattern

Painting by Charlotte Fung Miller and Kimberly Sau Wai Miller.

Padauk, 11" (279mm) high.

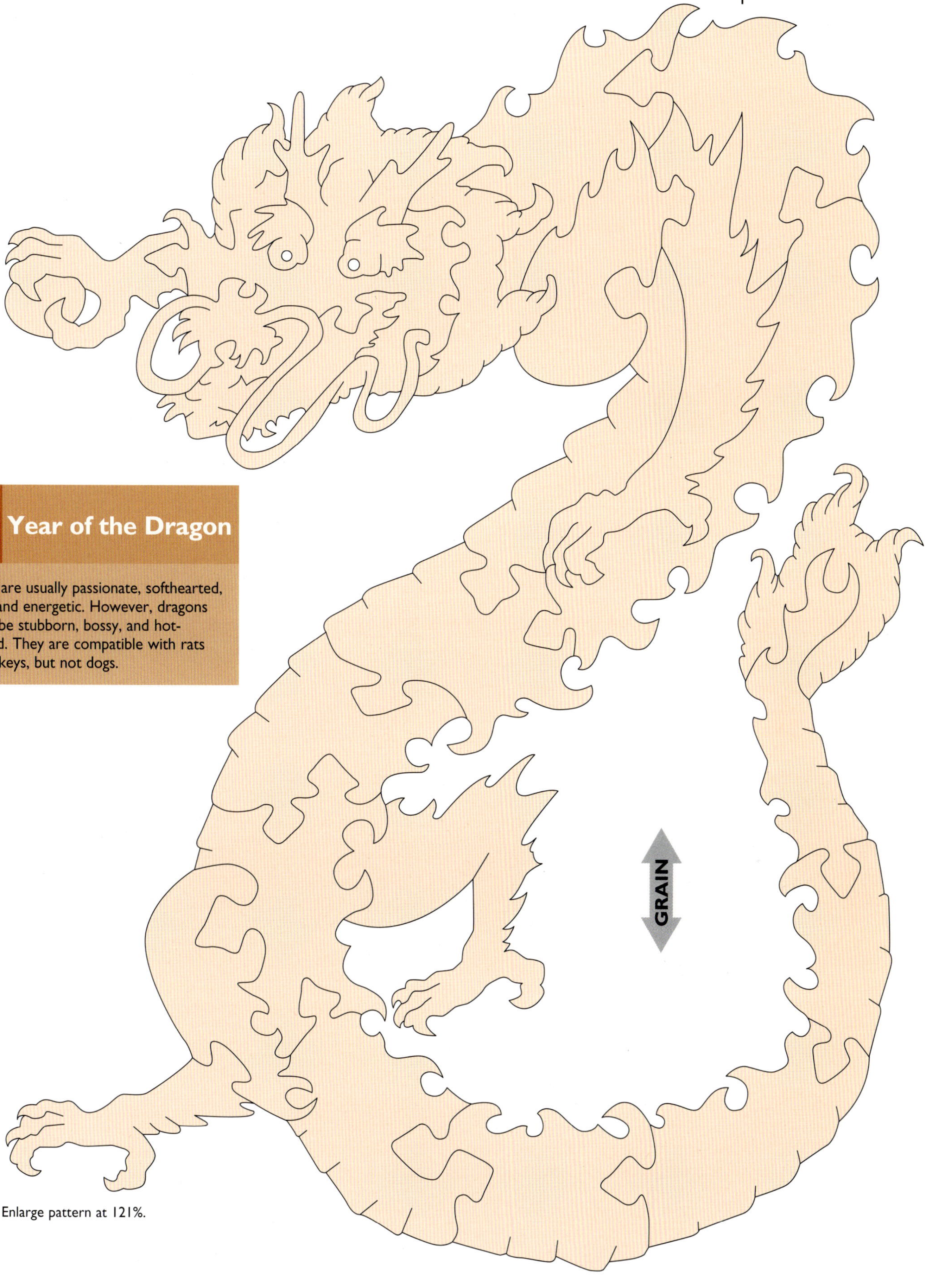

龙 Year of the Dragon

Dragons are usually passionate, softhearted, healthy, and energetic. However, dragons can also be stubborn, bossy, and hot-tempered. They are compatible with rats and monkeys, but not dogs.

Enlarge pattern at 121%.

The Eastern Zodiac — Easy Pattern

Painting by Charlotte Fung Miller and Kimberly Sau Wai Miller.

Bocote, 5" (127mm) high.

蛇 Year of the Snake

Snakes are usually wise, beautiful, and amiable. However, snakes can also be strong-willed, vain, and high-tempered. They are compatible with oxen and roosters, but not pigs.

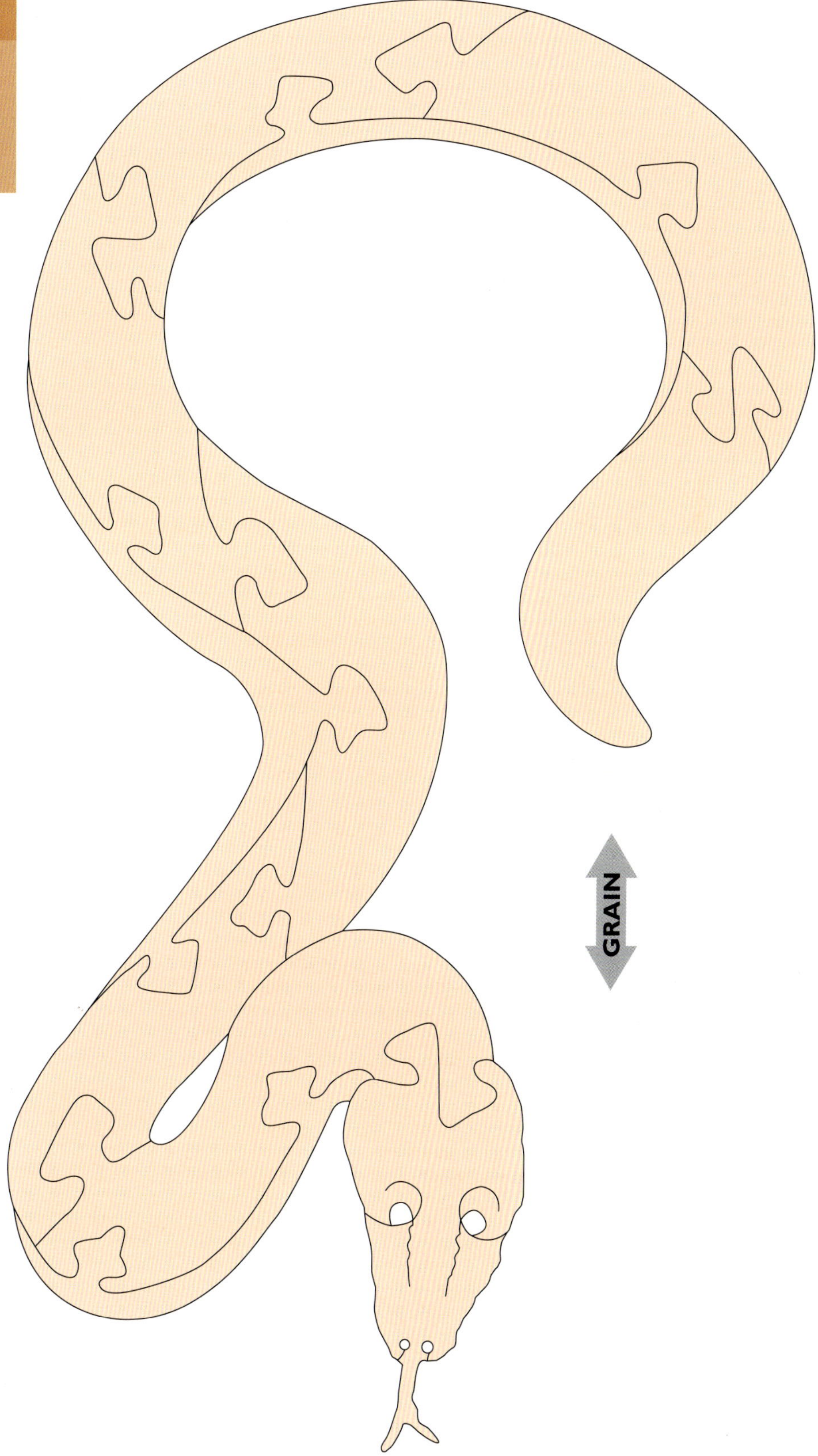

The Eastern Zodiac — Intermediate Pattern

Painting by Charlotte Fung Miller and Kimberly Sau Wai Miller.

Honey locust, 7½" (190mm) high.

羊 Year of the Ram

Rams are usually elegant, nurturing, and creative. However, rams can also be pessimistic, lazy, and careless. They are compatible with pigs and rabbits, but not with oxen.

Painting by Charlotte Fung Miller and Kimberly Sau Wai Miller.

Unknown wood, 7" (178mm) high.

猴 Year of the Monkey

Monkeys are usually intelligent, cheerful, and detail-oriented. However, monkeys can also be condescending and easily discouraged. They are compatible with rats and dragons, but not tigers.

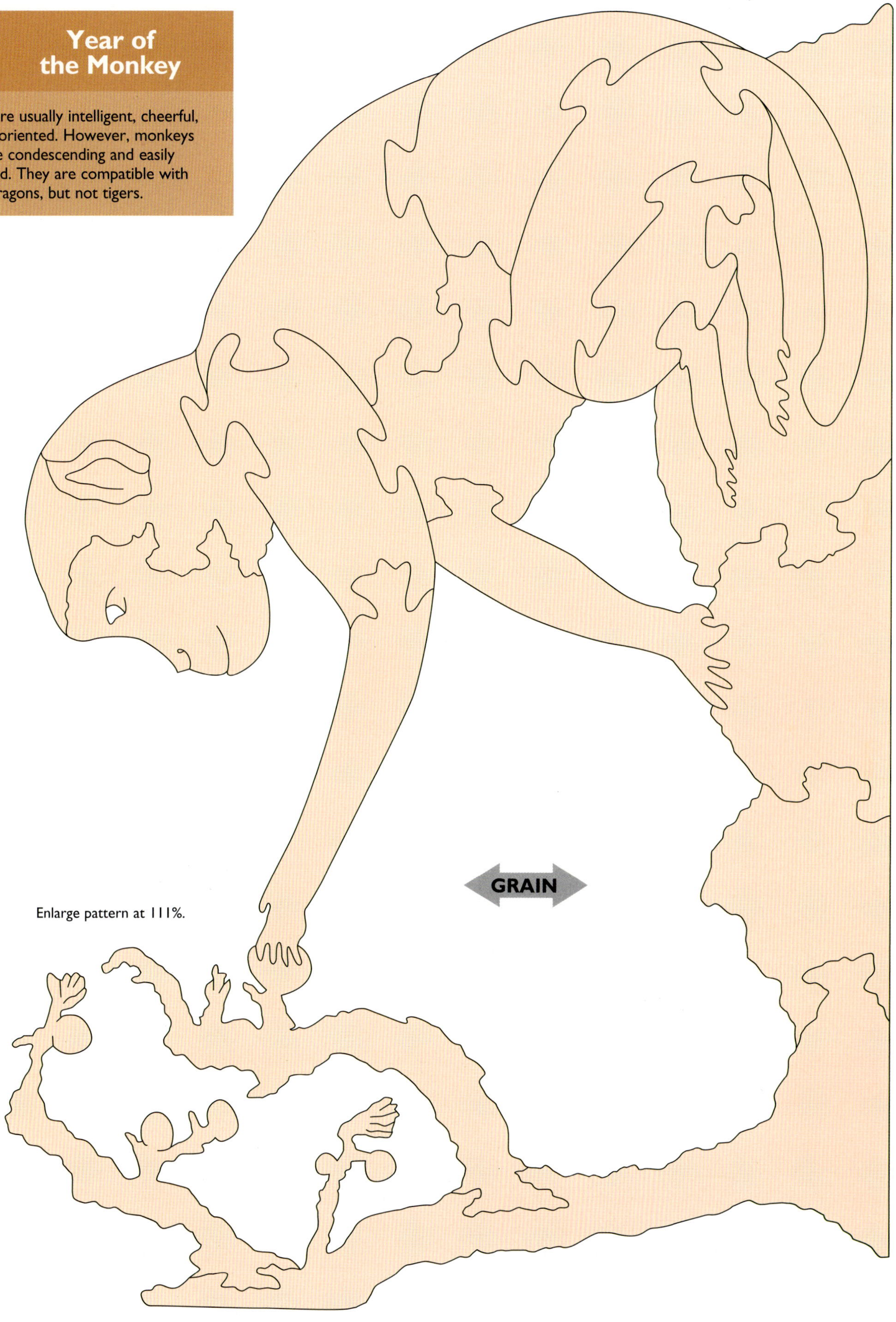

Enlarge pattern at 111%.

The Eastern Zodiac – Advanced Pattern

Painting by Charlotte Fung Miller and Kimberly Sau Wai Miller.

Bubinga, 8" (203mm) high.

鸡 Year of the Rooster

Roosters are usually hardworking, charming, and adventurous. However, roosters can also be blunt, eccentric, and cynical. They are compatible with oxen and snakes, but not rabbits.

Painting by Charlotte Fung Miller and Kimberly Sau Wai Miller.

Hububalli, 7" (178mm) high.

狗 Year of the Dog

Dogs are usually loyal, honest, and helpful. However, dogs can also be argumentative, selfish, and judgmental. They are compatible with tigers and horses, but not dragons.

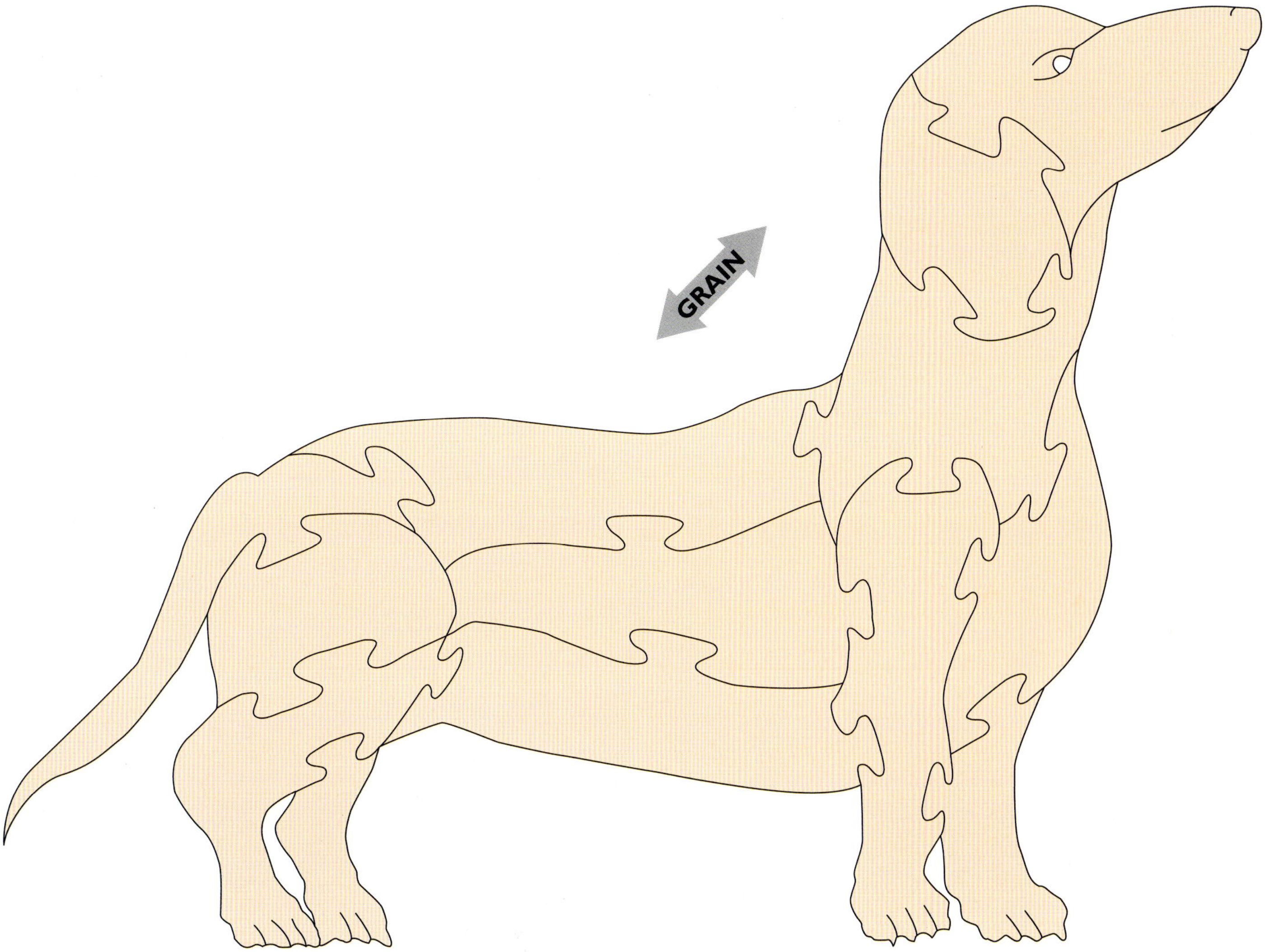

The Eastern Zodiac — Easy Pattern

Painting by Charlotte Fung Miller and Kimberly Sau Wai Miller.

Peroba rosa, 5" (127mm) high.

猪 Year of the Pig

Pigs are usually chivalrous, self-reliant, and generous. However, pigs can also be hedonistic, snobby, and pig-headed. They are compatible with rams and rabbits, but not snakes.

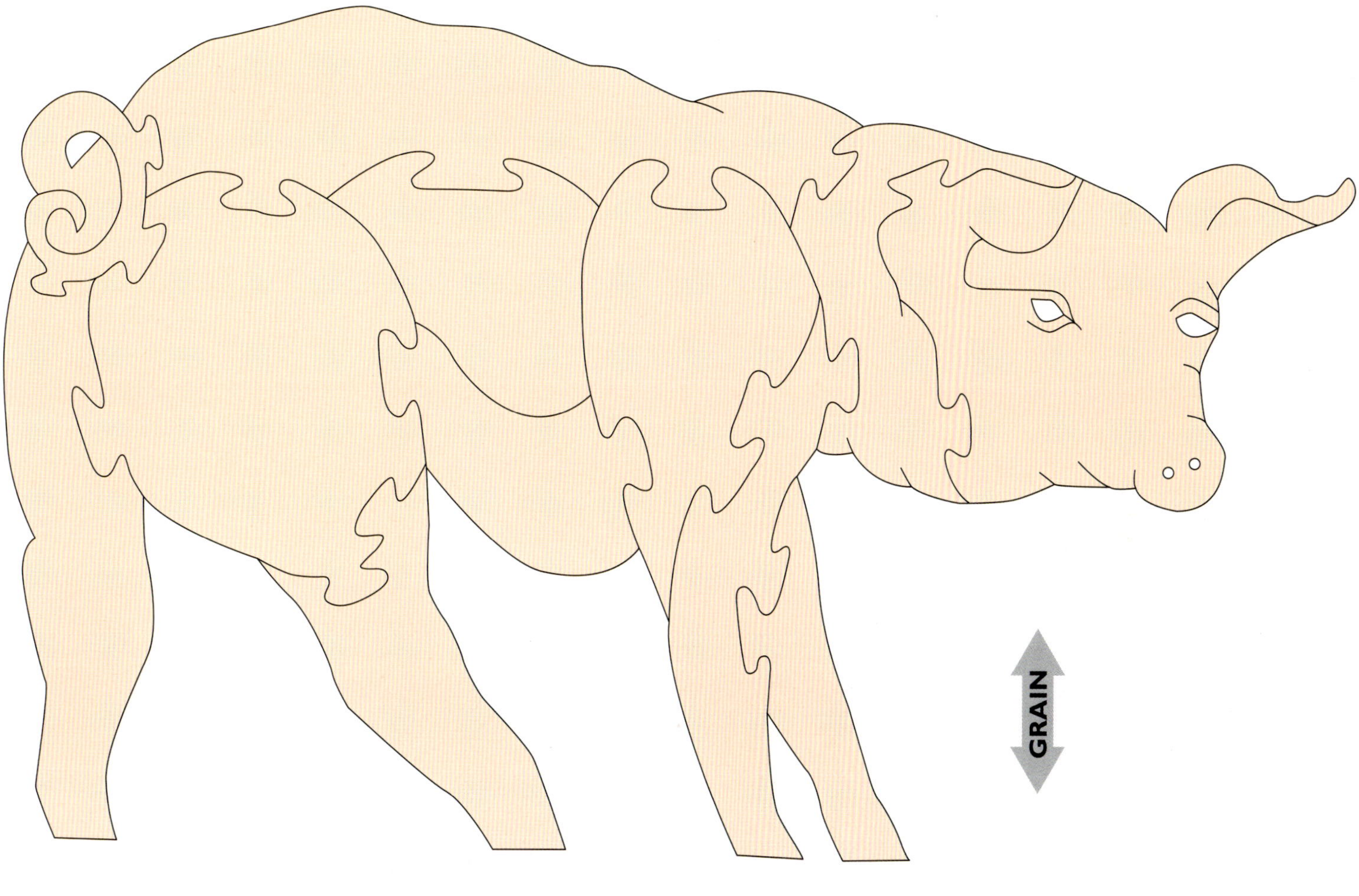

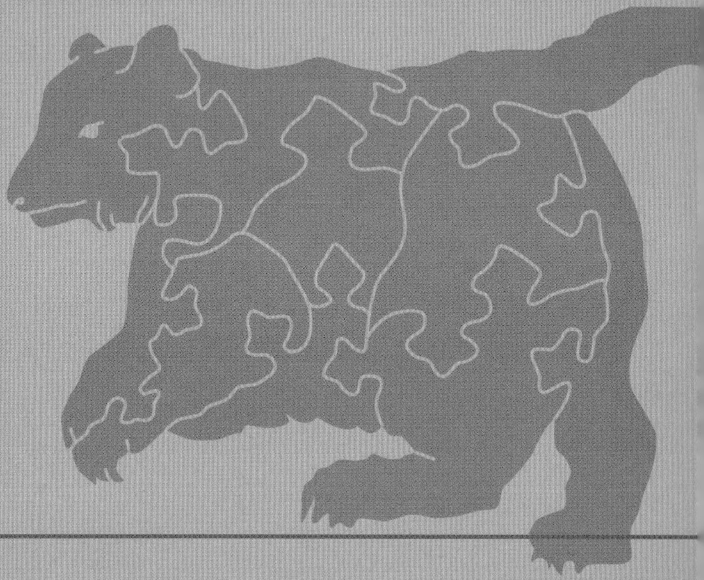

3 Constellations

Every culture in every part of the world has made pictures out of the star patterns in the night sky. For example, what we now call the Big Dipper was known to ancient Romans as the Seven Plowing Oxen; Babylonians as the Wagon; northwest Europeans as the Plough; Egyptians as the Bull's Hind Leg; Sioux Indians as the Skunk; and East Indians as the Hog's Jaw. Today, astronomers recognize 88 constellations. The six puzzles on the following pages represent six of the most popular and easily found constellations in the sky.

Each puzzle includes more than just a pattern and photo of the completed project. A beautiful historic star map, created in the 1600s by Polish astronomer Johannes Hevelius, is also shown for each constellation. Finally, the Greek or Roman mythology for each constellation is included.

Note: Read *The New Patterns in the Sky: Myths and Legends of the Stars*, by Julius D. W. Staal, for more interesting information about the stories of the constellations in cultures around the world.

Note: It was common for early astronomers to draw their star maps from a viewpoint outside of the celestial sphere, whereas today our star maps reflect a viewpoint from inside, as seen from Earth. Please note that the images from Johannes Hevelius' star maps will appear to have reversed star patterns and are placed as they appear in the sky.

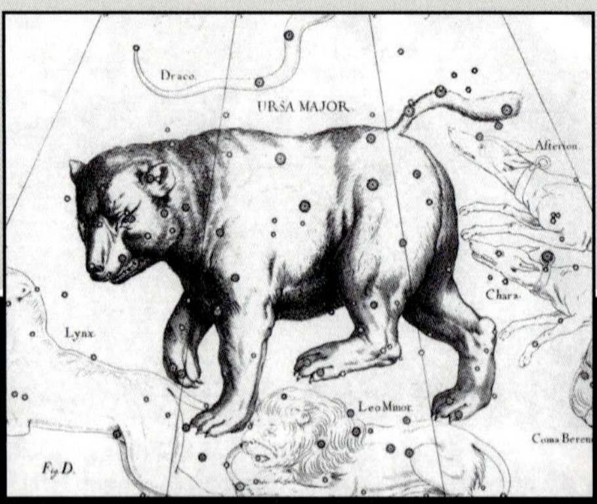

Walnut, 5" (127mm) high.

Ursa Major (Big Dipper)

I chose Ursa Major—the Great Bear—because it's probably the most recognizable of all the constellations. We know it better as the Big Dipper. The two stars at the front of the Big Dipper are the pointer stars to Polaris, the North Star. Polaris is part of Ursa Minor, the Little Bear or the Little Dipper.

In mythology, Ursa Major tells the story of Callisto, a beautiful huntress, and Jupiter. One day, Jupiter saw Callisto sleeping in the forest and seduced her. When Juno, Jupiter's wife, found out that Callisto had borne Jupiter a son, she turned Callisto into a bear. After many years of living as a bear, Callisto was hunted by her own son, Arcas. A sympathetic Jupiter intervened by turning Arcas into a bear, seizing both bears by the tail, and flinging them into the sky, where they became the Great Bear and the Little Bear. The force with which Jupiter pulled their tails stretched them into an unnaturally long shape.

Whereas Ursa Major is the Big Dipper to us, it has been seen as many other things to many other cultures over the centuries, as discussed on page 75. Isn't it amazing what the mind can do?

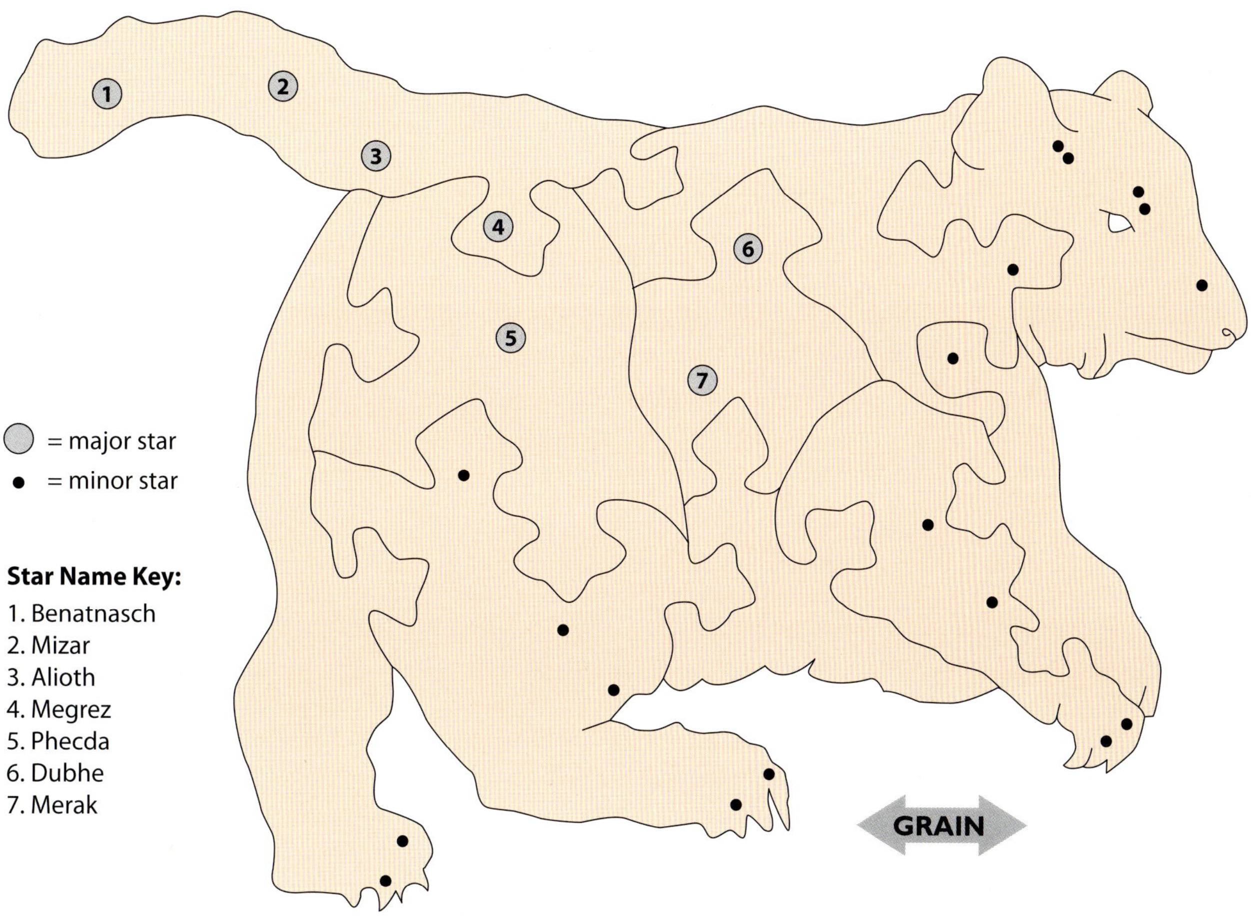

◯ = major star

• = minor star

Star Name Key:

1. Benatnasch
2. Mizar
3. Alioth
4. Megrez
5. Phecda
6. Dubhe
7. Merak

Constellations — Intermediate Pattern

Birch, 9" (229mm) high.

Orion: the Hunter

Orion is my favorite constellation. As a small child, I could lay in bed with my head on the windowsill. I watched Orion in spring as it rose over the hill. The shoulder and knee stars are bright and the belt can often be seen on a clear night. Betelgeuse, Bellatrix, and Rigel are three stars in this constellation you might have heard of. The Orion Nebula, M42, can be seen around Orion's sword. Orion was often imagined as holding a shield in his left hand. As far as I know no one ever put a dragon on it, but after all, this is my design!

Orion was a great hunter who had the reputation of being so tall he could walk through the deepest water without getting his head wet. There are many versions of Orion's story, most having to do with his boastfulness. In one story, the gods send a scorpion—Scorpio—to kill Orion. Now they circle the skies, chasing each other. It is also said that Orion is fighting Taurus the bull, which is adjacent to him.

The ancient Egyptians saw the stars that make up Orion as Osiris, the Egyptian God of Light. Osiris was seen as starting his journey up the Nile to the River of Heaven. Their imaginations incorporated stars below the constellation into the boat in which he was standing.

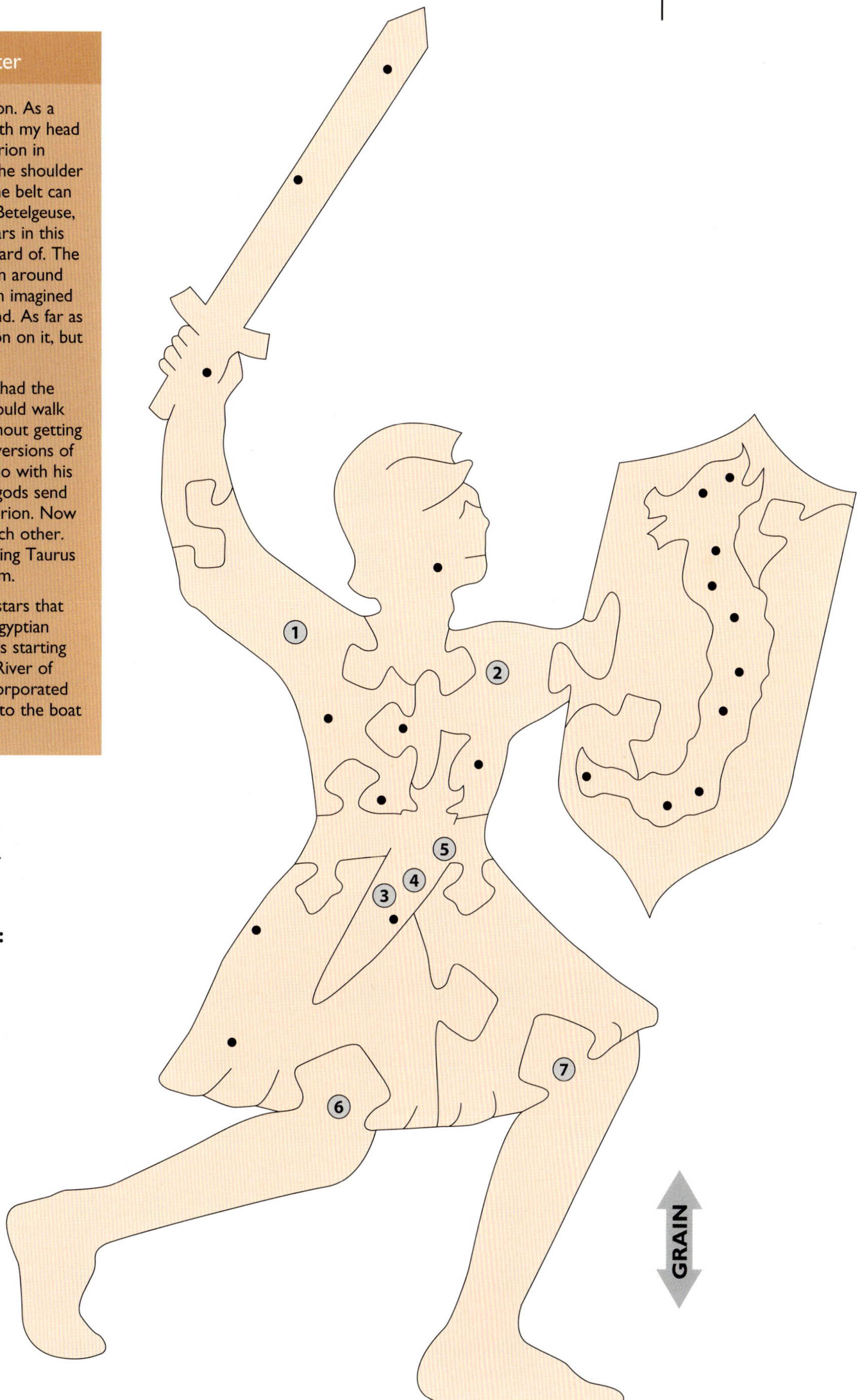

○ = major star

• = minor star

Star Name Key:

1. Betelgeuse
2. Bellatrix
3. Alnitak
4. Alnilam
5. Mintaka
6. Saiph
7. Rigel

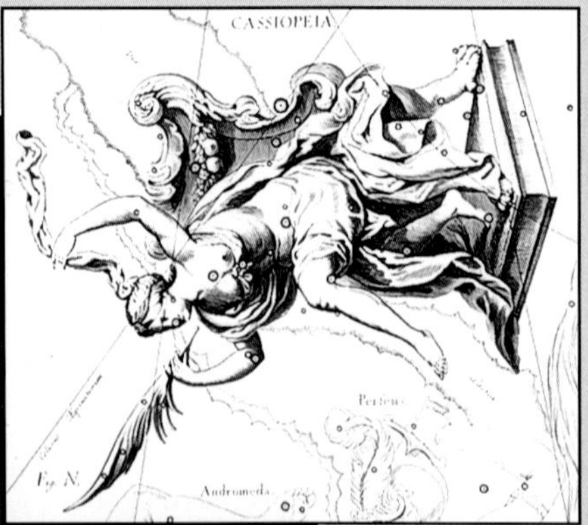

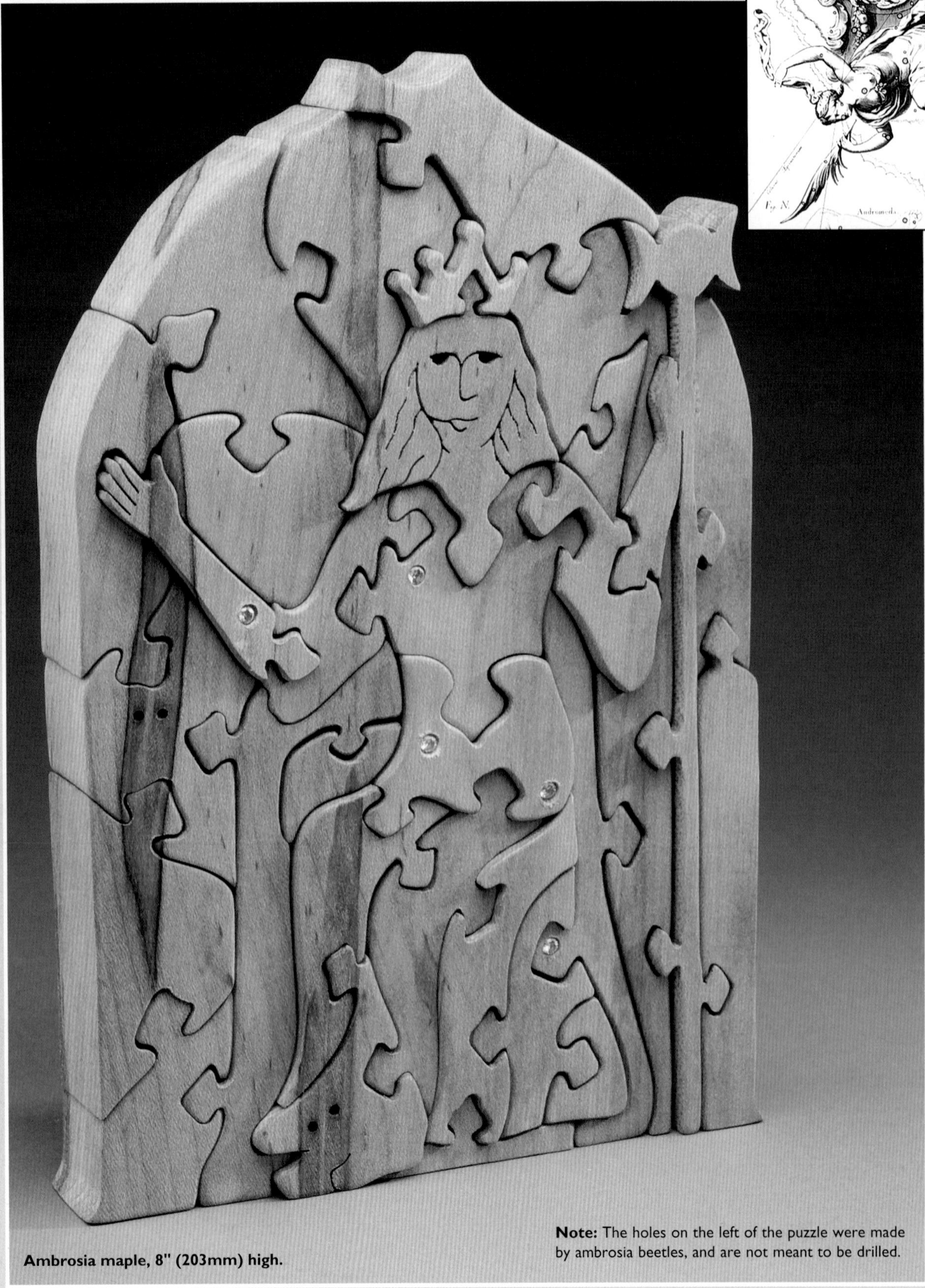

Ambrosia maple, 8" (203mm) high.

Note: The holes on the left of the puzzle were made by ambrosia beetles, and are not meant to be drilled.

Cassiopeia: the Queen

Cassiopeia is also easy to spot. She's the sideways, irregular W. If you follow the pointer stars beyond the North Star, you'll go between Cassiopeia and Cepheus (page 83).

In Roman myth, Cassiopeia was a beautiful queen. By bragging she was more beautiful than Juno, Cassiopeia began the chain of events that continues in the stories of the next three puzzles. After these events took place, she was condemned by the gods to travel forever around the North Pole, upside-down half the night. The story continues with the next constellation.

● = major star

Star Name Key:

1. Caph
2. Schedir
3. Cih
4. Rucba
5. Segin

GRAIN

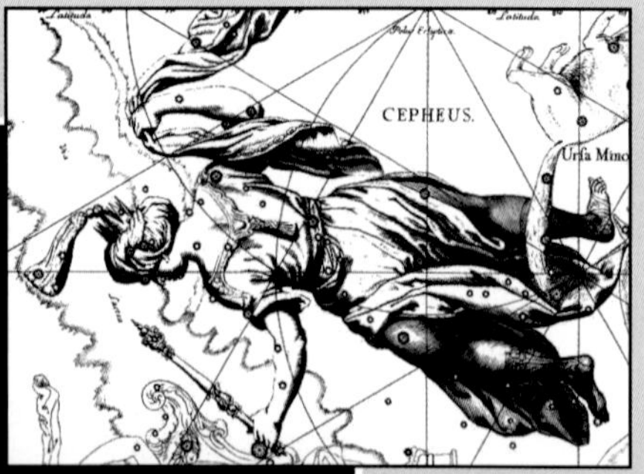

Ambrosia maple, 9" (229mm) high.

Cepheus: the King

In Roman myth, Cepheus was the king who was married to Cassiopeia. His queen is next to him in the sky. Not only was his wife in trouble with the gods, but also his daughter, Andromeda. The story continues with the next constellation.

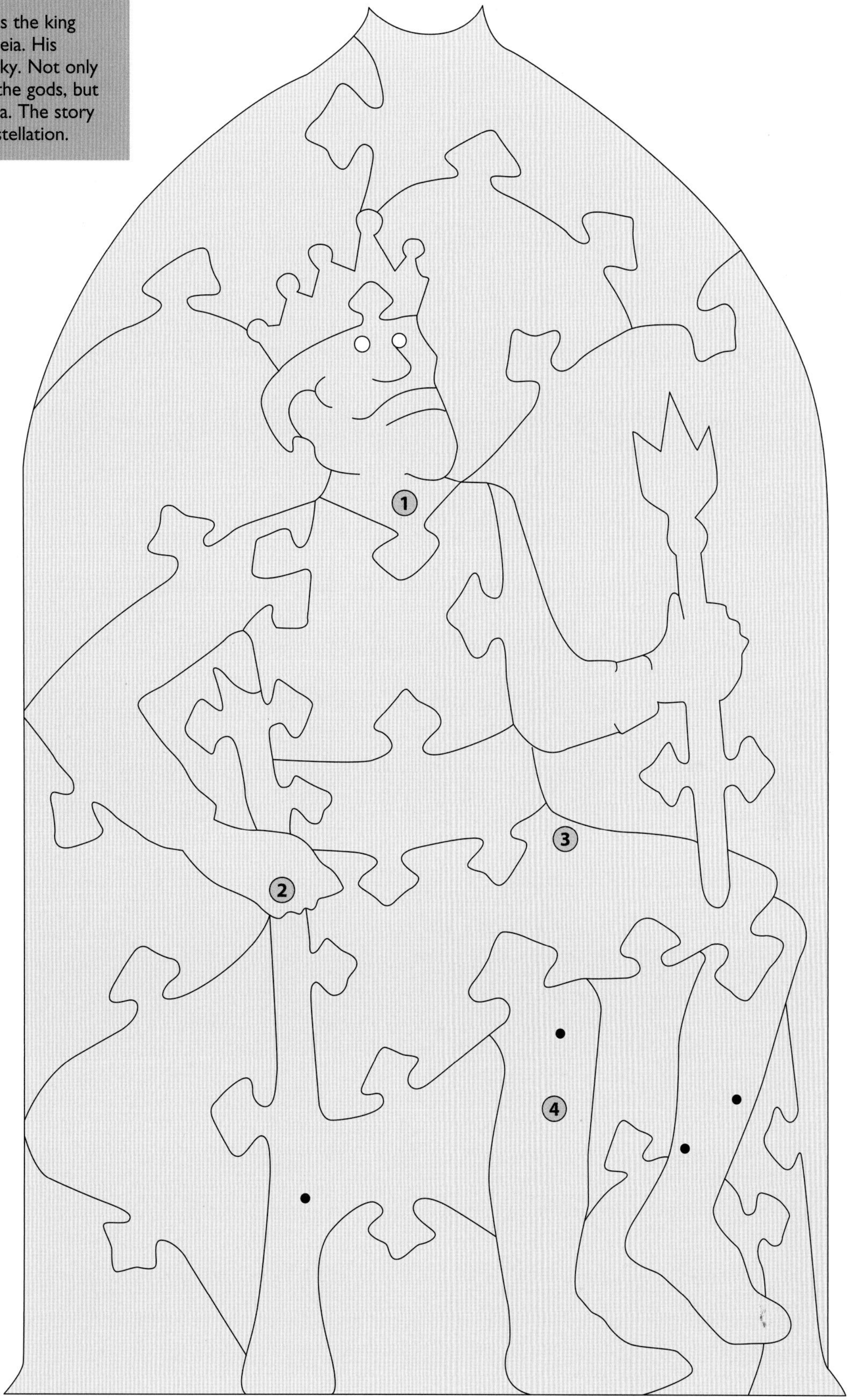

◯ = major star

• = minor star

Star Name Key:

1. Erral
2. Al Kurah
3. Alfirk
4. Alderamin

GRAIN

Birch, 7½" (190mm) high.

Andromeda: the Princess

Because of Cassiopeia's bragging, Neptune, the God of the Seas, created a sea monster called Cetus, which devoured people and their beasts at unpredictable times along the seashore. When King Cepheus consulted the oracle to see what could be done, he was told he would have to sacrifice his daughter, Andromeda, to Cetus. Left with no good options, Cepheus led Andromeda to the water's edge, where he chained her to a rock to be sacrificed. The story, perhaps the original soap opera, continues with the next constellation.

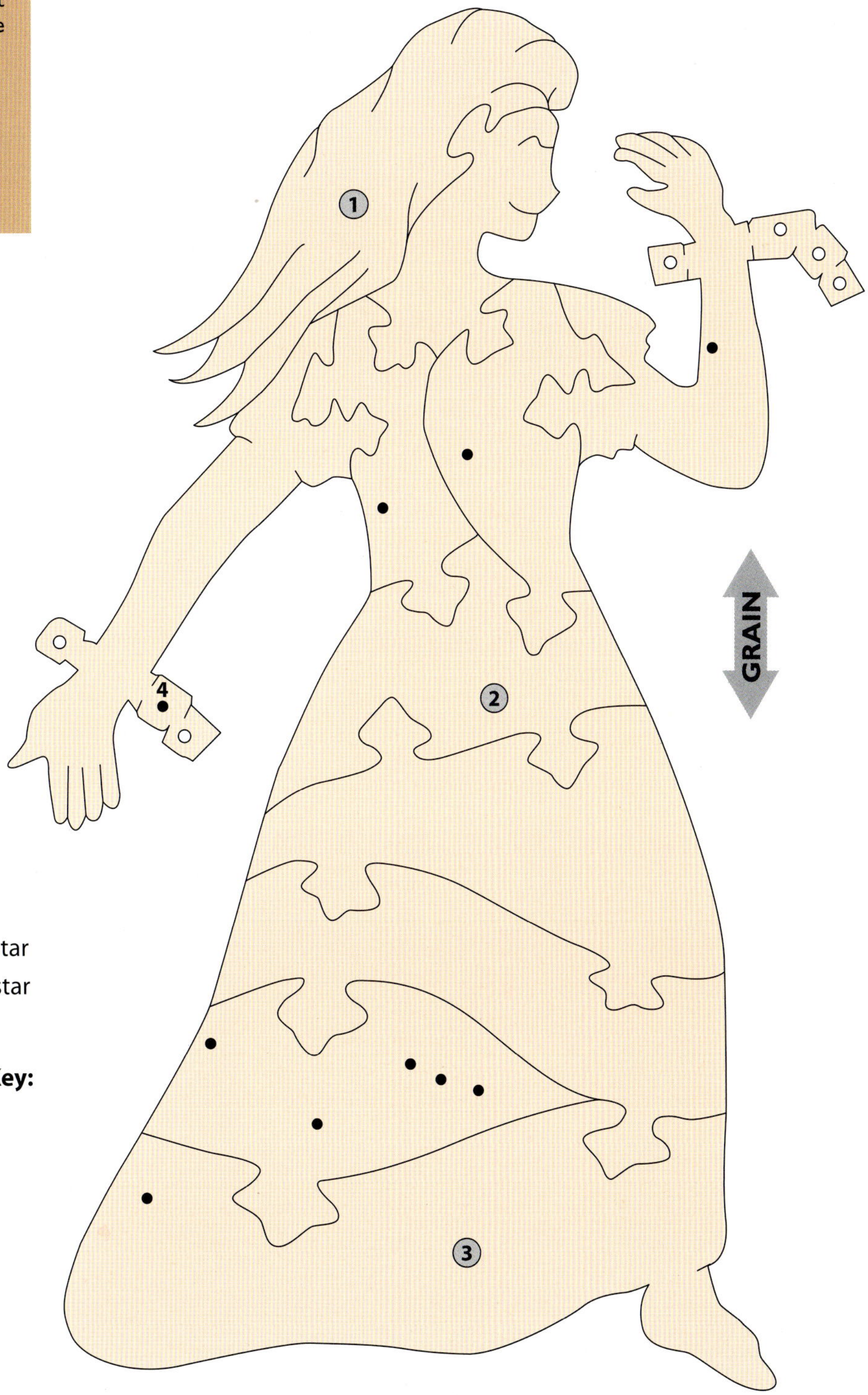

◯ = major star

● = minor star

Star Name Key:

1. Alpheratz
2. Mirach
3. Almech
4. M31

Birch, 8" (203mm) high.

Perseus: the Hero

Perseus was on his way home after slaying Medusa, a monster with snakes for hair and a gaze that could turn anyone to stone. (The puzzle version of Perseus holds Medusa's head in his hand. She's not having a bad hair day; those are serpents growing out of her head!) Just as Andromeda was being chained to the rock, Perseus flew over on his winged horse. Perseus said he would rescue Andromeda if King Cepheus would allow him to marry her. Cepheus agreed, and Perseus took his position near the rock. When Cetus appeared, Perseus leapt from his hiding place, pulled Medusa's head of out of a bag, and turned the sea monster to stone. Perseus broke the chains that bound Andromeda to the rock and married her. (Don't you just love happy endings?)

The Perseid meteor shower falls from the direction of Perseus around August 10 each year. Another interesting star in Perseus is Algol, the eye of Medusa. This star seems to fade and brighten over a cycle of several days. Ancient people believed that this was the eye of the Medusa blinking. We know now Algol has an orbiting companion star—when it passes between Earth and Algol, the star dims.

Note: The star clusters in the tip of the sword were left off the puzzle shown.

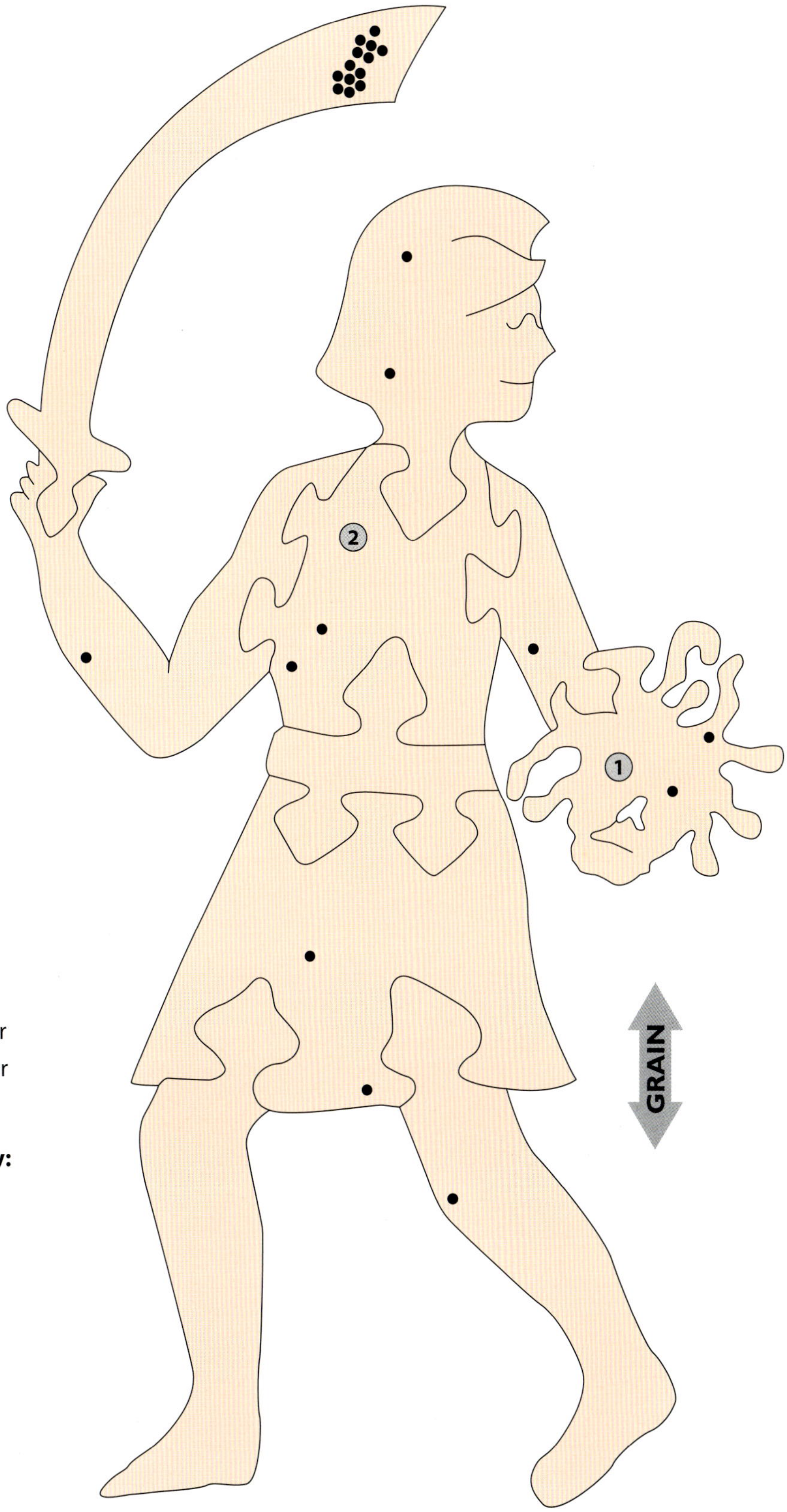

◯ = major star

● = minor star

Star Name Key:

1. Algol
2. Mirfak

Appendix

Tools & Techniques

Safety

It should come as no surprise that cutting thick wood generates a lot of sawdust. Nor should it come as a surprise that breathing sawdust is not good for you. In my workshop, I have a dust collector and an air cleaner. The dust collector picks up the large particles and many of the small ones. Even if you have a dust collector, however, the air in your workshop will still have many tiny particles floating around. My air cleaner is mounted on the ceiling and removes a high percentage of the particles that the dust collector misses. Beyond using those two machines, I wear a dust mask that uses replaceable filters.

Eye protection is mandatory! I was in fifth grade when I got my first pair of glasses. Because I can't find a company that makes the kind of safety glasses I want and because I can't see well enough to work without my regular glasses, I use my regular glasses for much of my woodworking. However, my regular glasses have titanium frames and hardened lenses. When I'm sanding, I wear side shields. These translucent plastic devices slide onto your frames and keep flying particles from hitting your eyes from the side. They are available at most vision centers. Whatever type of eye protection you use in your workshop should include side shielding.

While visiting my dental hygienist recently, I noticed she was wearing a slightly oversize clear plastic shield to protect her eyes. They looked like glasses with a long plastic pipe-cleaner frame. I immediately recognized them as a solution to my eye protection problem. The product name is "Googles," and she gave me one to use. I took off the frame piece and slipped it in behind my glasses. It works just fine. I found at least one company online (Dental Disposables, International) that makes/supplies them. I wrote to them to find out how a non-dentist might buy them. However, they did not reply. I suggest you make friends with your dental hygienist and hope for the best. If you don't need prescription lenses, use safety goggles.

You'll also do a better job of cutting and be safer if your saw has a good, efficient dust blower. This device blows the dust away from your cut line. I call this a safety issue because, before I had a blower, I reached up without thinking to wipe the dust away from the cut line and cut myself! Don't let it happen to you.

Also, make sure to have enough light in your workshop to see what you're doing. I have two swing-arm lamps (widely available, oddly enough, at office supply stores) mounted on my saw. These lamps come with clamps, and you can usually find somewhere to attach them if you don't have a mount for them on your saw. I find I can cut longer with light coming from both sides. This setup also eliminates shadows and a good amount of eyestrain. You need adequate light for everything else you do in the workshop, too.

I also wear a hearing protector. If you're into serious woodworking, you would be well advised to at least invest in a mask, eye protection, some type of hearing protection, and possibly a dust collector.

A word about saws

I have owned four different brands of saws and have used several others. Although it's easier to cut anything with a great, big, expensive, production-quality saw, all of these patterns have been cut with a cheap, rickety, difficult machine. Just keep practicing.

Squaring the blade

I have never seen a saw with a truly accurate degree gauge. Be sure your table is square to the blade; get an engineer's square and use it to level the table. Check your squareness if you have trouble cutting a true vertical.

To check that the blade is square to the table, lift the saw arm up as far as it will go and place the square next to the blade. Place a white piece of paper behind it to allow yourself to see the blade and the edge of the square as clearly as possible (below). If the edge of the square is not parallel to the blade, your table is not level. Adjust the table accordingly.

Square the blade with an engineer's square.

You may also want to check that the blade is moving in a true or nearly true up-and-down motion. Expert scroll sawyer Steve Malavolta suggests moving the blade to the "up" position, and then placing a flat piece of material next to the blade. Slowly move the blade to the down position and watch to see if the blade gets closer or farther away to the material. If the blade doesn't move, you're in good shape. If it does move side-to-side, use your saw adjustments (if your saw has them) or try shimming at the blade clamps as necessary. I adjusted my blade after reading Steve's tip and I am getting better cuts.

Cutting on the line

Cutting on the line is important on the outer edges of the puzzle. It is vital for facial features and is desirable on the inner cuts.

If you wobble on the outside edge of a puzzle, you can either re-cut it or ignore it. If you get off the line while cutting any of the features, stop. Look at where you are and see if the cut can be saved. If it can, try to do so. If it can't, throw the puzzle out and try again.

On the interior (or interlocking) cuts, accuracy is not terribly important. What is important is the shape of the key. In order for the key not to pull out of the keyhole, the head of the key must be larger than the neck of the key. It also must be balanced so that there is material on both sides of the neck.

PARTS OF THE KEY

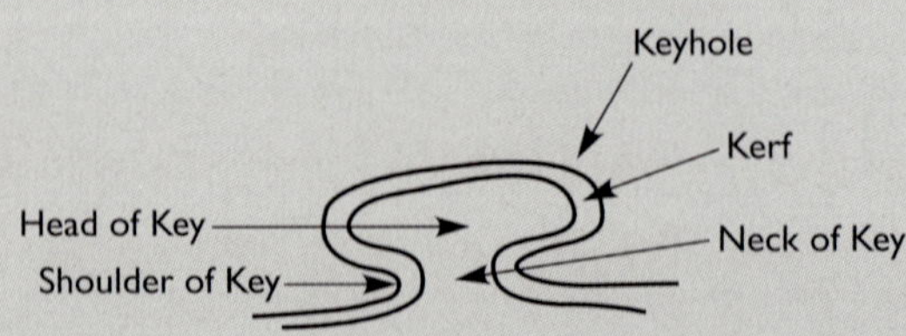

On puzzles with large pieces, there is a lot of room for error. Smaller pieces require greater accuracy. See drawing above, which shows how to cut the key, as well as how it is designed.

Preventing burn marks

Burn marks are a frequent problem when cutting light-colored hardwoods. After gluing the pattern in place, cover the pattern with a clear plastic sealing tape. The heat generated by the friction of the saw blade causes the plastic tape to melt. This lubricates the cut and almost eliminates burn marks.

Clear plastic sealing tape is available at department stores, office supply stores, grocery stores, and lumberyards, just to name a few. You want 2" (50mm) clear plastic tape without the Mylar strands. By following this tip, I can even cut purpleheart without leaving (many) burn marks.

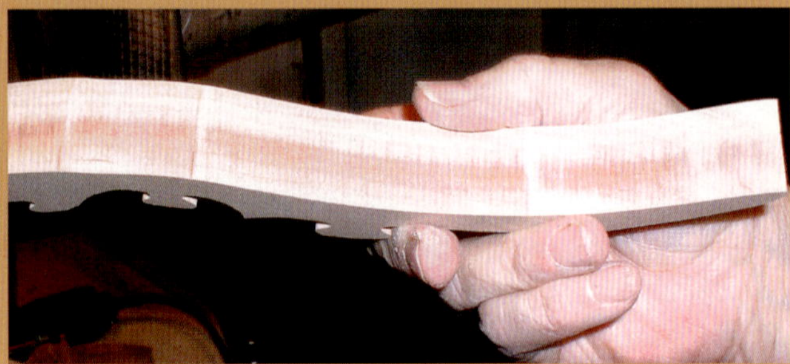

I cut this cherry puzzle without covering the pattern with plastic tape. This piece is external, so I had quite a bit of sanding to do to get rid of the burn mark.

Pattern classifications

Three-dimensional puzzles are much more difficult for young children than flat puzzles with the same number of pieces. With three-dimensional puzzles, there are small muscle control issues involved. That's why I advise people not to give a more complicated puzzle to a young child. Also, note that most of the puzzles in this book contain swallowable pieces! It is critical that none of those puzzles are within the reach of children under the age of three. Here's the easy way to tell: if a piece will pass through the hole in a roll of bathroom tissue, it can be swallowed. To handle and not swallow the pieces or lose the gems, a child needs 1) to be over the age of three, and 2) to not be rough with his/her toys. Drill the holes to represent the star pattern, if you like, but eliminate the gems and wires if it seems wise to do so.

Easy – The puzzles marked "easy" have fewer pieces and uncomplicated faces.

Intermediate – These puzzles have more detail cuts in addition to the facial features.

Advanced – Most of these puzzles have complicated faces, which demand a great deal of control.

Hardwoods

Hardwoods are naturally beautiful. As a lover of hardwoods, I have a natural aversion to painting them. They're beautiful in their own right. Besides that, hardwoods occur naturally in a variety of colors. Why cut a tiger out of a piece of pine and then paint it when you can cut it from a tiger-colored wood complete with stripes? But more about that later.

The harder the wood, the less chip-out you get. The structure of hardwoods appears to be more uniform than softwoods. Uniform density makes your cutting more consistent. You'll spend less time overall and end up with a more pleasing result.

The increased density also results in a surface that can be more easily sanded smooth. To paraphrase something we said in our first three books: silky translates into sales at an art show.

Where can you buy hardwoods?

Look in the yellow pages of your phone book under "Lumber, Hardwood." Ask your woodworking friends. Check out the ads in your favorite scroll sawing or woodworking magazine; some of these magazines may be available at your local library, specialty woodworking retailers, or hobby shop. Keep your eyes open as you drive through unfamiliar areas. We're on the road a lot driving to and from shows. We found one of our best and most reliable suppliers in Ohio that way. If you have access to the Internet, use a search engine to find "Hardwood Lumber Dealers."

To get started using hardwoods at a lower cost, ask your hardwood lumber dealer if he has any "shorts" available (see the Lumberspeak tip box on page 92). None of the puzzles in this book are very big. Just make sure the piece you choose is long and wide enough to do the job (also make sure the grain is running the way you need it to run).

For more information about wood, your local public library is a source that's available to everyone. If you have a home computer, the door to almost unlimited information is open to you. This is especially true if you also have access to the Internet. Check the Resources section for a list of good wood sites.

How do I choose wood for color and cutting characteristics?

I try to choose woods suitable for the item being cut. For instance, I cut Leo in Osage-orange or satinwood. I also pay attention to my customers. Moose usually sell best in black walnut. Evidently, most people think that's the right color for moose. Almost every puzzle has a wood in which it sells best. I know I might not have found the perfect wood for a particular pattern yet, and that knowledge keeps me searching for new and wonderful woods.

Appendix

Most of my puzzles are cut in native North American hardwoods. Cherry, walnut, and maple are widely available in this area. Cherry appears to be the wood of choice (at the moment), but walnut and maple are always popular. I also use a smaller amount of butternut, aspen, and catalpa. These woods are locally available in limited quantities.

I buy almost all of my North American hardwoods from a local sawmill. The state of Wisconsin publishes a booklet about our lumber industry, which lists all the sawmills and what they specialize in. Check with your state—there are little sawmills all over the country.

From time to time, I use sweet gum, mesquite, sassafras, and other regionally grown woods, all of which have advantages and disadvantages. Many truly beautiful woods, including many exotics, are too hard (or almost too hard) to cut with a scroll saw. When I run across a new species, I pick up a board. If it's heavier than a similar-sized board of hard maple, I put it back.

I cut the Libra puzzle from macacauba, which has a marked contrast between the colors of the heartwood and sapwood.

I always look at every board I buy. I'm looking for color and figure. I want the richest color for that species and any figure I can find—wavy, quilted, fiddleback, etc. (You will need to learn "Lumberspeak." See the tip box at right.) I also like the contrast between heartwood and sapwood—see the photo above of Libra with its carrier after sanding and finishing.

Lumberspeak

- **Grain Figures.** "Figured," "fiddleback," "quilted," "wavy," "flame crotch," "rowey," etc. are terms that really mean that the grain of the wood is not straight. Any figure is the result of some stress that the tree was under while growing.
- **Hardwood and softwood.** "Hardwood" only means "deciduous tree," or a tree that loses its leaves in the fall. It has nothing to do with how hard the wood is. Some hardwoods are softer (less dense, lighter) than some softwoods.
- **Maple and oak.** Lumber people know only two kinds of maple, hard and soft, and only two kinds of oak, red and white. This is the case regardless of the fact that there are 20 or 30 species of each.
- **Hardwood sizes.** Hardwoods are sold by the quarter inch, i.e., ¾" (three-quarter) (19mm), 5⁄4" (five-quarter) (32mm), etc. This is the unplaned measurement. Planing reduces the thickness of the board. If you go to specialty lumberyards, they will plane to your specifications, for a price.
- **Skip planing.** Hardwood lumber dealers will usually skip plane your lumber if you ask them to do so. This type of planing will give you the thickest board possible. However, you will have to pay more attention when you sand to make sure everything is smooth.
- **Kerf.** This refers to the wood taken out by the saw blade.
- **Shorts.** Lumber less than four feet in length. Lumberyards often end up with cut-off ends, which their regular customers cannot use. They typically sell shorts at lower than usual prices.

What are some of the advantages and disadvantages of various hardwoods?

The biggest disadvantage of hardwoods is price. Most hardwoods are more expensive than most softwoods. However, if you're using hardwoods, you don't have to buy 87 kinds of paint, learn to paint, or spend the time painting your projects.

The biggest advantage of hardwoods is beauty. With careful selection, you can produce a beautiful puzzle.

There is one characteristic of hardwoods that's both an advantage and a disadvantage: the hardness. It takes longer to cut a puzzle in hardwood, but the finished piece is stronger. This is a great selling point for children's toys (and for puzzles for clumsy adults).

Practice Pattern

Occasionally, I teach scroll sawing at my local Woodcraft store. Many of my students are just getting started, so I developed a practice pattern for them. If you can cut this entire pattern, you can cut anything in this book.

Appendix

Pattern Inspiration

I created the patterns in this book in a variety of ways. Some were inspired by images I found in books and star maps; some came out of my head; some were adaptations of patterns I had already created; and some of them came from things I saw in real life. You, too, can design your very own patterns using any of these ideas. Stay on the lookout for interesting and different designs—you never know where you'll see one! Keep a scrapbook of your ideas so when the time is right, you'll be able to scroll fantastic new creations. Make sure you tweak the design so it is truly your own, and don't forget to give credit to your inspirations.

Thanks to the following sources for their inspiration in creating the patterns in this book.

Atlas Celeste, by John Bevis, made available on CD by Michael Oates and the Manchester Astronomical Society in England.

Chinese brush paintings, the twelve animals, by Charlotte Fung Miller and Kimberly Sau Wai Miller.

Stories and Lore of the Zodiac, by M. A. Jagendorf.

The Children's Homer: The Adventures of Odysseus and the Tale of Troy, by Padraic Colum, illustrations by Willy Pogany.

The Constellations: Stars & Stories, by Chris Sasaki, illustrations by Joe Boddy.

The New Patterns in the Sky: Myths and Legends of the Stars, by Julius D. W. Staal.

Chinese Years

Rat	1900	1912	1924	1936	1948	1960	1972	1984	1996	2008	2020
Ox	1901	1913	1925	1937	1949	1961	1973	1985	1997	2009	2021
Tiger	1902	1914	1926	1938	1950	1962	1974	1986	1998	2010	2022
Rabbit	1903	1915	1927	1939	1951	1963	1975	1987	1999	2011	2023
Dragon	1904	1916	1928	1940	1952	1964	1976	1988	2000	2012	2024
Snake	1905	1917	1929	1941	1953	1965	1977	1989	2001	2013	2025
Horse	1906	1918	1930	1942	1954	1966	1978	1990	2002	2014	2026
Ram	1907	1919	1931	1943	1955	1967	1979	1991	2003	2015	2027
Monkey	1908	1920	1932	1944	1956	1968	1980	1992	2004	2016	2028
Rooster	1909	1921	1933	1945	1957	1969	1981	1993	2005	2017	2029
Dog	1910	1922	1934	1946	1958	1970	1982	1994	2006	2018	2030
Pig	1911	1923	1935	1947	1959	1971	1983	1995	2007	2019	2031

You should be aware that the Chinese New Year does not fall on January 1; unlike the Western calendar, the Chinese calendar is based on the phases of the moon. The Chinese New Year falls on the date of the second new moon after the winter solstice (how's that for more information than you wanted?). For that reason, the Chinese New Year can fall as early as January 21 and as late as February 19 on our calendar. In 2009 (the Year of the Ox), the Chinese New Year fell on January 26.

Index

Pattern index

More Great Project Books from Fox Chapel Publishing

Animal Puzzles for the Scroll Saw—Expanded 2nd Edition
By Judy & Dave Peterson

Newly expanded to include 20 new animal puzzle patterns! Step-by-step instructions for making Mama Rabbit with Babies along with 50 great patterns.

ISBN: 978-1-56523-391-1
$17.95 • 128 Pages

Fantasy & Legend Scroll Saw Puzzles
By Judy & Dave Peterson

25 easy-to-follow instructions for puzzles depicting fabled creatures from Greek mythology and other storied traditions.

ISBN: 978-1-56523-256-3
$14.95 • 80 Pages

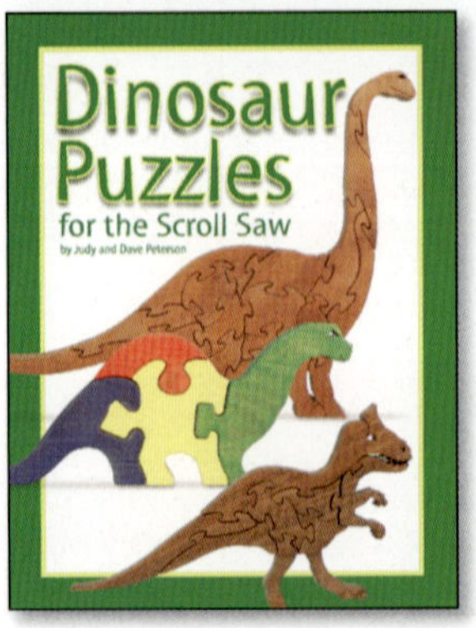

Dinosaur Puzzles for the Scroll Saw
By Judy Peterson

30 easy-to-make and fun puzzle projects that will keep children—and adults—cheerfully engaged for hours.

ISBN: 978-1-56523-184-9
$14.95 • 80 Pages

Wooden Puzzles
By Editors of *Scroll Saw Woodworking & Crafts*

More than 30 of the most popular puzzle projects selected from the pages of *Scroll Saw Woodworking & Crafts*.

ISBN: 978-1-56523-429-1
$17.95 • 96 Pages

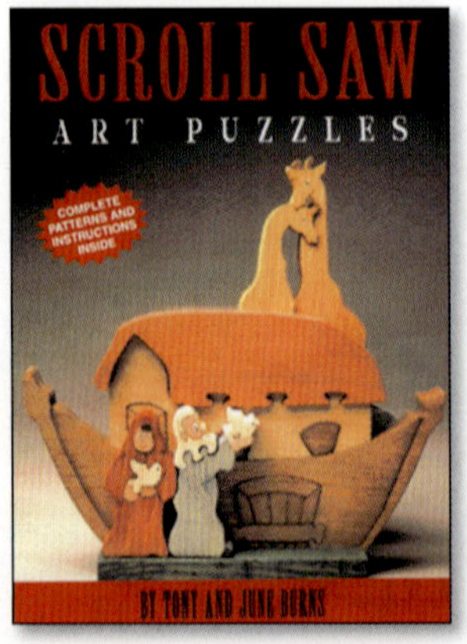

Scroll Saw Art Puzzles
By Tony & June Burns

Includes step-by-step cutting and painting demonstrations plus 32 fun puzzle projects including flowers, animals, whales, Noah's ark, and more.

ISBN: 978-1-56523-116-0
$14.95 • 88 Pages

Intarsia Woodworking Projects
By Kathy Wise

From a celebrated intarsia artist comes 21 original full-size patterns. Included are step-by-step tutorials.

ISBN: 978-1-56523-339-3
$19.95 • 80 Pages

SCROLLSAW Woodworking & Crafts

In addition to being a leading source of woodworking books and DVDs, Fox Chapel also publishes *Scroll Saw Woodworking & Crafts*. Released quarterly, it delivers premium projects, expert tips and techniques from today's finest woodworking artists, and in-depth information about the latest tools, equipment, and materials.

Subscribe Today!
***Scroll Saw Woodworking & Crafts:* 888-840-8590**
www.FoxChapelPublishing.com

Look For These Books at Your Local Bookstore or Woodworking Retailer
To order direct, call **800-457-9112** or visit *www.FoxChapelPublishing.com*

By mail, please send check or money order + $4.00 per book for S&H to: Fox Chapel Publishing, 1970 Broad Street, East Petersburg, PA 17520